A NICE LITTLE EARNER

Jason Cook

Based on the true-life events of a gangsters' runner in

London's, underworld.

Part Three of "There's No Room for Jugglers in my Circus"

Part Four is on its way.
("Cocaine THE DEVILS POWDER")

All books available at www.amazon.co.uk

http://www.authorjasoncook.com/

https://www.facebook.com/profile.php?id=100006763187069

https://www.facebook.com/pages/Jason-Cook/30808437618?ref=hl

JASON COOK

First published in Great Britain by Jason Co

All paper used in the printing of this book has been made from wood grown in managed, sustainable forests.

ISBN: 978-1910-667-071

Printed and bound in the UK

A catalogue record of this book is available from the British Library

Cover design by Paul Joel

Graphic Artist www.pauljoel.com

This novel is based around a true story line, and some true events. However all characters in this book have been changed and any resemblance to actual persons mentioned, living or dead, is purely coincidental as some have been changed to Protect the innocent.

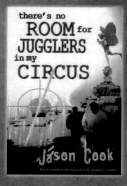

Acknowledgements:

I am grateful for the love and support of so many people during the process of writing this book, so I would like to extend a huge thank you to all those that believed in me and have helped me with regards to my writing.

In particular I must mention and say thanks to My Mum and Dad, Vivian, Matt, Mark, Dolly, Steve, Bones, Sam, Elaine, Lisa A, and Lisa S. Big thanks also to Sharon at Kilburn market stall Bonzo, Lewis, Tom, Begs, Dave C, Frank D, Pauline K, Jamie, Peter M and Tim, Alan (AKA DJ Mad All the best old school DJ I have ever met - enough respect to all of acid.) Andy and Helen and also Alf, for some of the best times of my life and for giving me his time and help and encouragement to fulfil our dreams. Also thanks to Sim, for the support he has showed me and my family not forgetting M. Chudzz and a massive thanks to Author Georgia Melaris, for the editing. Also to my good friend Tracy Coggins for her help and support throughout with not only my writing but in other parts of my life too. Special thanks goes to my dear children for understanding the time it takes to write a book and for giving me that time.

CHAPTER 1

Being back in England for the funeral after everything that had happened, I was now being taken for enquires as to what had happened to Mandy and the depot job. When I think back, after leaving Paddington police station, something wasn't quite right but I just couldn't work it all out right then.

Too much had already gone on in a very short space of time; burying Mandy and Johnny and being pulled in for questioning. My mind was all over the shop and the money stolen from the depot was well gone.

I thought it best to stay away from the Firm for a bit as the police were so close to us. I just needed to keep my head down and try and sort it out. I decided to get back in the gym and train hard. All the cocaine-fuelled days and the paranoid long nights had brought me down a few pounds and I was starting to get out of shape and so I hit the steroids. Training hard was a good thing for me. As they say; *it's survival of the fittest*. I had too much on my mind with everything that had happened back then. Well wouldn't you if you were a dead man nearly two or three times over?

Once by the Columbians, but that was sorted by the depot money. Twice, by the Russians' mafia man for the money we owed him for the bank bond that was given to Mr B which was sussed by the police when they had been caught.

Johnny had kindly sorted that Russian for me by shooting him down in no-man's land in Barbados without him even knowing he had done so for me. The situation we were in at that time with owing him a shipment of cocaine or the bond money back! That stress had gone when a bullet had left Johnny's chamber. So I had had a result.

Johnny had killed him for a revenge killing of his mum and step-dad we had found out there was a method to his madness after all and for a moment we all assumed Johnny had just flipped, lost the plot. The third near death moment for yours truly happened when Johnny came after me for getting Mandy killed, but then he had gotten himself taken out by the police.

So, I was safe for a while, as it seemed, because everything was on an even keel or at least as even as my world gets! The reality was that we still owed Mr Nice £1 million as he was still expecting us to come back out to Spain with the stolen money that Old school and I said we had and he had pulled strings to get it cleaned for us. Then I nearly got myself banged up as I had been pulled in by the police for association at the funeral, but I had been given a good brief by Mr Nice. This lawyer worked his magic and I had been let off with no charges. There's always a loop hole in the law if you dig deep enough.

After all, I didn't know anything illegal had gone on so they were barking up the wrong tree or that's what I told them. They had no choice but to let me go after no comment and I didn't know anything about that. I thought things would have calmed down a lot by now but the police were still sniffing around and were definitely still on our case, making things a lot more difficult for all of us.

Now, they had found information on the Firm from the people they arrested at the funeral when raiding their drums and of course while doing so, they had uncovered other links to other criminal things that had gone down; or were about to go down? With the photos they had taken from the funerals they were ready to bring anyone and everyone in and question them for more leads.

It was clear to the police that the Firms and the people in them were somehow connected to each other, but as Mr Nice wasn't present, they couldn't place him in the middle, although they really wanted to. They had to have the number one. They knew he was involved somewhere in the food chain, right at the top of this very aggressive food chain but they simply couldn't prove it.

The police really wanted the top man. They knew if he went down for a long time it would mean the end to this whole criminal organisation and for some of the police, an early retirement.

After Johnny was shot, I thought if I stayed away from the Firm and the people in it, my life may just get a little bit easier. Mr Nice was being nice for once. After all, he had spent a day organising meetings for us with his Arab friend to get the money on to the oil rig and out of England. This is how it should have gone down. We were going to take the dollars on to an oil rig using a speed boat and then have it picked up and flown safely to Dubai. Boom ... Sounds easy yeah?

Unfortunately, we had no money as Mattie the Mac had got nicked with a vanload of our dirty cash! The Columbians had taken the rest of it for what I had owned them for the cocaine deal that Mr B had been nicked on.

Look, that's the scenario, we were just following Mr Nice's orders. Otherwise, Mattie would get one right between the eyes when they had phoned us before or just after they had shot Mandy. They weren't fucking around and had proved it on several occasions when trying to find me and Old School while we were lording it up in Spain, thinking we had loads of money at our disposal and were now amongst the untouchables.

The blame was on both of us really because now, we were all skint again. He couldn't say one thing about the whole fuck up as he was the one who told me to hand it all over thinking we still had a van load of stolen cash.

Mr Nice had sent over his good friend that he had now made his new number one guy once he knew Johnny had been taken out of the equation. So, he had arranged a meeting and everyone was told to be there, but more about that later.

So, me getting out, or getting away from the Firm for a bit was easier said than done because my absence from this pretty fucking important meeting would have been well noticed by the types who you don't want to notice you! Factor in my being pulled in by the police, my not turning up, would lead to uncomfortable questions from those in the underworld. The seed of doubt would have been planted in peoples' minds; the wrong peoples' minds.

The meet was held at Camden Palace in Camden town. This was an old haunt big in the height of the rave scene. So, at the meeting I had now been introduced to other villains and Britain's most wanted, and of course to now Mr Nice's new number one who was about to introduced to us this fella called Malcolm.

I was told by Old School that I should attend for my own good. Like I say *I'd kinda figured that one out for myself.* I walked into the club and was told to sit down at the table watching man after man join it and that's where I met Malcolm. He looked like some fella out of the Sopranos and had a slight South American accent. He was rough round the edges and had evil eyes. He had replaced Johnny who was now gone.

Malcolm was now in his position; Mr Nice's number one boy, second one down the line in this villainous chain. But for some reason the Firm wasn't the same and didn't feel as strong knowing Johnny wasn't around. Even if he had wanted to kill me, you simply had to respect Johnny, he had that kind of presence. Malcolm didn't seem to have the same scare factor about him, or the air of confidence.

Everyone knew Johnny was a killer, but Malcolm … Well, no one knew about him and his capabilities because no one I knew had witnessed any action from him, but if Mr Nice says he's the number one guy, then he is number one.

There must have been a good reason for it. Who was I to test him anyway? It's hard to keep away from the Firm or this sort of people once you have friends who are involved and well-connected in such villainous circles. And, the twenty-nine grand I got from the diver that had got away from the cocaine deal in Southend hadn't lasted long. I remember that the diver that had got away after I bought the last key of cocaine off him; well we never saw him again … (Well not yet anyway!) So, I would see myself back in the Firm; it was my fate.

You may think why get involved again since if I had found my way out? But I hadn't really. I was just laying low. We were all laying low now these things had gone down, and if I had taken a step back at that point, then I may not have been in the Firm and would have got a glimpse of reality. Then things might have been a lot different.

As always I was blinded by the lights and by a fistful of fifty pound notes, sure as hell I would soon be led like the rats in The Pied Piper story back into the realms of skulduggery! Straight back into the underworld of London.

One moment of weakness and before long you're rolling with the nines again. Old School had asked me to come to this meeting and I couldn't say no, after all we had been through together, so we had to show a little bit of respect and loyalty to each other. Fuck me; you can justify anything to yourself if you try hard enough!

Therefore, before long, I was face-to-face with the gangsters again, running money and drugs all over London and picking up guns and other bits and bobs! I knew very soon I'd be skint again and looking for the next nice little earner to pop up. You are always chasing the dream thinking you're Scar Face.

Talking of Scar Face, if you think these things only happen in the movies, well you're dead wrong, they were happening and to us here, now. These things do happen and are still going on today just not with me being involved in them; I'm one of the lucky ones!

At this time, I still had a few quid kicking around to keep me afloat. As you know, with easy money comes easier spending. So, when Old School had asked me to come on this meet I knew it wouldn't be long before we would be all working again, and not long till a nice little earner was soon to come up in the Firm. Or would it? After losing all the stolen money.

Things were getting a lot worse. It's not all glitz and glam like you see in the films, let me tell you. It's more swings and roundabouts and a little bit of luck if the truth be told. As we had empty pockets; the stolen money from the depot job had gone wrong, and Mr Nice had taken advantage of the whole situation. Old School and I had now found ourselves in with him, whether by plan or just circumstance, we'll never know. It had all happened just out of coincidence with regards to the stolen money from the depot that was taken for payment by the Colombian hit men.

They had come looking for me whilst I was out in Spain and they had killed Mandy and nearly Mattie the Mac in the process. Mr Nice saw that there was a golden opportunity there if he acted fast and he did, he had taken it with both hands. He was now planning and scheming behind our backs. As he knew, if he could get the outstanding money back from the Columbians then it would be a nice little earner for him.

He now wanted back what was overdue from the van that the Columbian hit men had taken from me and Old School for the debt and of course for his time in trying to clean it.

He assumed we were millionaires after we showed him the local newspaper to confirm our dastardly deeds and how we had pulled this depot job off. Mr Nice had thought if he speculated he would accumulate with us as he thought he was quid's in. How could it have gone so wrong for us?

Ignorant of the whole fucked up situation - Mr Nice had his hopes up, already thinking he too would make a million pounds as promised if he helped me and Old School move and clean the money! Not knowing that two days later we were in fact skint again without a penny to our names and that I had got Mandy killed in the process! But he knew now that I had had her killed and he knew Johnny would be wanting my blood sooner or later.

The police and the Columbians cleaned us right out as they had taken the van-load of money from right under our noses. So, that's how Mr Nice knew that there was a lot more money in the van than I had initially owed the Colombians. So, he thought it was his if he could get it back. Without anyone knowing a thing, because he didn't let on. The reason he hadn't been around was because he was in fact getting ready to try and get the contact number for the Columbian Don the 'Grim Riper.'

To go out to see the 'Grim Reaper,' which the Colombian Don had said his name was at the time of me and Old school meeting him in String Fellows club. The night when me, Old school and Mr B had set up the fateful Cocaine deal, the cause of so much disarray!

The 'Grim Reaper' and his family, as you can imagine, were well connected by marriage to the Colombian cartel. Mr Nice already had a few quid, not loads, but a bit, nicely tucked away, but it seems it wasn't enough. That's what I couldn't work out. Why? With the money these top gangsters and villains allegedly had around them, why would they continue to take risks like that?

Why not stop doing what they were doing when the money was good? I guess it must be the world's most potent drug? It's about power, and the type of life style most people can never really contemplate!

But seriously, the odds are you keep doing it and one day you will end up getting caught and losing the lot. It's the law of averages. Even the untouchables get caught sometimes. These top gangsters had more than most by now, or was that all a front too? There's a lot of paranoia in my game, don't know if you can pick up on that? I had heard at the meeting that a large shipment of cocaine had fallen off one of Mr Nice's lorry pales in France, and that he and they, had put quite a lot of money in on it.

The fella they were working with had also tried to smuggle immigrants over without Mr Nice and the others knowing about it. They had jumped out from the back of the van in France and left the bloody back door open and unlocked. Who hired these amateurs I'll never know! Anyway, as the driver suddenly hit the brakes, the cargo of tins filled with cocaine, labelled as tomatoes, slid forward and then back again. It came flying out the back doors and spilled all over the road. What's a driver to do? Course he's gonna make a run for it, right?

The lorry was left stuck there in the middle of the road for the police to find. So, there was a ton seized by the French police, which left one or two of these money men out of pocket and pointing the finger at each other because now, there was a large hole in Mr Nice's wallet.

Who was going to cop the bill for the next lot to try to get some money back? Sometimes, in this game it's all about being lucky, or unlucky as the case may be. Losing a lump sum like that is hard to swallow so, I guess they needed to try to get some of the stolen money back from the Columbians. Say what you want, this shit is business and all businesses need to balance the books!

As you can now see, not every big drug deal that goes down ends up landing on our streets ready for the eager nostrils. Someone, somewhere still needs to pay for it, when it goes pear-shaped.

It was no use in blaming us for the fuck up, but now there wasn't any for us even if Mr Nice had wanted to blame us; it wasn't our fault. When we finally came clean to Mr Nice he quipped.

"I can always rely on you two to fuck things up." What he didn't tell us was this: he thought he could take what he now thought belonged to him for his time and trouble out of the outstanding; the money that the Columbians had taken.

Mr Nice wanted every penny back that was over the debt paid back to him from the Columbians, and rightly so, but it wouldn't be shared with me and Old School this time round. It was all for himself. Me and Old School wouldn't see a penny and we wouldn't even know!

Looking back to that day, when Old school and I had gone out to Spain sharpish to try get the stolen money out of the country. Leaving London for Spain, thinking we were millionaires, not thinking for one minute we would arrive back to England with less than ever. It's not often you can blow sixty million in ten fucking days.

Well, it can be done as we have just proved. Whilst Old School and I were still in Spain trying to get the money sorted to get it moved over there and cleaned, we were with Mr Nice living the life of Riley. Everything was on his tab of course, as our money was still stuck in London stashed up in the vans with the straw bales covering them. Or, so we thought!

Mr Nice at that time thought we were loaded, so he was liberally dipping into his own cash for us, no questions asked! For once, we did not have to put our hands in our pockets for anything. It's funny how the tables turn when you have a few quid behind you, or at least others think you do.

Everyone wants to be your friend again and all is forgiven when they think you have a few quid as they believe you're dangerous with it. As life is now cheap, pay a crack-head a grand or less and he will kill or maim or hurt if needs be for the cause …

Then everyone thinks you're loaded and it's all good again. The women, they sort of see a new beam of light in you and they are soon walking around following you like you have the fucking Lynx effect.

But hey, money helps me believe that; 'no money, no honey.' They assume if they were with you then things would also be all good for them too. They had no clue it was real bad as Old School and I had managed to fuck up, once again, with the stolen money. It was gone, every last single penny, all gone. Well for a split instance we were self-made millionaires and everything was rosy.

The fellas had been paid that had done the job and had gone well into hide out mode in other hot countries. The rest was all downhill.

Then it had all gone wrong at Mandy's funeral, I will go into that in more detail shortly!

For now, all that matters is at this eventful funeral the police had photos of most of the Firm as they had a hunch Johnny wouldn't be able to stay away! Now they had released her body for us to bury.

So now, I had put that behind me. Life goes on.

I stopped reminiscing and tried to get my life back. I needed a job and wanted anything just to put some pound notes in my sky rocket (pocket). Like I say, the £29k I got from the diver was long gone. Out of this shared money from the key Mr B had given a few quid to pay off outstanding debts he still had with other villains that he also worked with. I had met them at the casino when I met Malcolm, but more about that in a second. Mr B had also given a little bit of money to his ex-Chrystal to look after; thinking he would have some money to come out to, but she had spent the fucking lot.

This left him skint as well, although he didn't know that yet; Chrystal had kept it hush hush as she thought he had enough on his plate being inside. So, inside he was okay with a tenner a week coming off for canteen. *How's your luck?* Chrystal had had enough of all this drug dealing and gangster's business. She had been mixed up in it for ten years and more. Mr B just kept his nose clean and was now just riding his bird out the best way he could in prison, ready for a chance of maybe getting parole.

I hadn't been in touch with Old School for some time and was just training at the gym, keeping a low profile before this new meeting. I had only read about the Firm in the newspapers; about the gangland killing of Mandy and the police killing of Johnny, and the breakthrough the police said they had on a big Firm in London.

I hadn't had any contact with them, including Old School and Mr Nice who was still at large trying to get a contact number for the Colombian. The papers could write what they liked. I thought not being involved meant I was also out the Firm. Well, the main players and Mr Nice were all trying to keep a low profile so it was for the best. It was hard trying to go straight having a criminal record. As it would play over and over again when I went for any jobs and still 12 years on I have to declare it or it holds me back in some suites. "Ah, Mr Cookster, come into the office. Take a seat. You seem the man for the job." Sound familiar? It was getting too familiar for me after having a criminal record and trying to get a full-time job and being on pub watch for 11 years after going down for selling cocaine and

E's and a little bit of puff and speed and any stolen things I could buy cheap . It seemed trying to go straight just wasn't happening. I would be branded for the rest of my life as a criminal. Not only had I done my punishment by being inside, but I would now be punished constantly. Even though it all started from one ecstasy tablet and one line of cocaine, The Devils Dandruff, which lead me to becoming a supplier for my own addiction; first recreational then every weekend and then, every day.

I remember one instance where I thought it was all going well for once in the interview for a job. But the interviewer then turned into Alan Sugar at the Last Question.

"Can you start Monday morning?"

"Yes."

"That's great. Look forward to working with you." We shook hands and he smiled, "Just one more thing Cookster."

"Yes?"

"Do you have a criminal record?"

"Err, well … Yes." Alan Sugared.

"You're fired."

"Sorry Mr Cookster, I'm afraid …

"Save your breath. I know the rest."

I left, shutting the door behind me.

The only people that would give you a job were the agencies and they were stealing half of your money before you even got it. There was no pension scheme at that time if you worked for them. So, as soon as the meeting came up and a job opened up in the Firm, you guessed it, I was their man. Old School knew it.

So did the rest of them, as a few of them had worn the same shoes before me and trod the same path when they had tried to get out the Firm. You know you're going to jump at the chance of getting some dirty cash when you have no money. Sixty-five pounds every two weeks from the dole don't buy you much.

Money talks in this life and the bills need to be paid somehow. I thought I wasn't hurting anyone and I wasn't pushing drugs. I was holding them and selling them to those who wanted them and using them myself. So, if more work came up in the Firm I would snap their arm off for it. Or else they'd say; *Look, we know you're skint. So take this and we'll see you in a couple of weeks,* Or, *Here's a few quid, pay me when you have it.* Then two weeks pass and they're phoning you up demanding it back, so, you have no choice but to work with them and do as they ask.

Now you're sitting there holed up with loads of speed, cocaine or E's or puff, that you would now put all your efforts in and try to sell and risking your liberty. Ringing round and telling everyone you worked with that you were ready. That you were back in business and had anything they wanted, come on, we all have bills to pay no matter where the money comes from.

I knew by selling drugs it meant I wasn't robbing or hurting anyone; only those that wanted the drugs. It was demand and supply. Basic business, simple economics, like I say it is what is and I am who I am, what can you do? We justify our shit don't we?

I was not standing outside pushing them on people. The only thing is that in a nine to five, not many people get hurt. The hours are good. The police aren't following you everywhere and the henchmen are not coming to kick your door in, or worse your head, while flashing shooters at you.

Your girlfriend, parents and friends are not looking for you and you're not looking over your shoulder for someone to rob or scam you or take your kindness for weakness. It's a cruel world out there, but it can be a lot crueller in these circles of skulduggery and that was my world.

When you're walking around with a head full of cocaine and you're in a right proper Charlie Daze most days of the week, things can and will only get a lot worse. Life can get on top of you very quickly. So, once an offer came my way for me to get back involved with the Firm, that was me, bang back at it.

This time round, I would take great caution not to get sucked in as much as I had done before. I would take care not to get caught by the police or end up in prison like I had when I was younger. Now I had proved myself to the Firm and have redeemed my worth well. I was also, kinda, debt free.

Those I owed money to were now either paid or dead, except for Mr Nice and technically I didn't owe him anything. This meant I could call my own shots. I was now a face with those that were in the know, but all for the wrong reasons, and I had now met and would soon be working with Mr Nice at the top of the tree. The villenairy world of London seems small compared to the other side of the world. London's true gangsters were ageing and things were changing fast.

I was older, wiser and I had seen what this gangster business was all about, and how most of them were just drug dealers. Not gangsters. Not real gangsters. The real gangsters were wearing pin-striped suits sat up safe in London's top hotels, living life, not trying to build a life, as they were settled living it somewhere out in Puerto Buenos while others controlled parts of London or its club life or other businesses that were a front for dirty cash made from the drug trade.

It's weird when I was dealing I always had money in my back burner and the milky bars were on me, but really, did I want to risk my life or waste it by making someone else rich at the cost of my own health, safety and the safety of my family and true friends not acquaintances?

I knew now that it was the gangster's runners that were more dangerous than the gangsters themselves. It seemed that the gangster's runner did all the dirty work, with a few thugs and mugs who caused the violence when needed.

This made the gangster look good or at least meant he himself wouldn't get nicked for it. It was a smart move on the gangster's part. In fact, it was a smart move having a runner in his pocket and also a few big henchmen on their payroll, and a trigger man which would make the Firm a force not to be reckoned with.

It also helped if they had a few quid behind them as then they could pay for people to be killed once told to do so, just like Johnny had done many times before. But he himself bit the bullet - what goes around comes around. As the saying goes, 'Why have a dog and bark yourself?'"

Get a few big monkeys, pay them peanuts and they do the work for you. Knowing that, and everything else I had learned, I knew, or thought I knew, that I could easily break away from the Firm's tentacles that were always pulling me back. As well as the unwanted thoughts that kept creeping back in to my mind. Thoughts that had haunted me for years. Why was I involved with the Firm? I thought if I just sell this last lot, I'll stop. If I just collect all the money I owe them, then I'll stop. If all the tickers come in today. I'll stop. I guess, tell yourself the same thing often enough, you start to believe it ... at this moment in time that was the type of stuff I simply had to tell myself.

I'll just do this last gram and … you got it, I'll stop. I'll just finish the last joint and then I can stop. I'll stop. I'll fucking stop! The battle goes on and on in your head. Once again, and if I'm more careful, the police can't catch me. Well, I'll just do it on special occasions now. Like every Saturday night.

Who was I kidding the police had more grasses on their books then I had punters. So, to ease the pain, you hit the cocaine. You think you can see more clearly once you have fed your hungry nostrils. You place the note next to the other lines that you have nicely prepared, ready, all in a row while you're sat there turning into Sméagol from The Lord of the Rings.

You look at the cocaine laid out in front of you, then you look at your reflection in the mirror staring back at you with big, bulging eyes and those whispering lips. Your jaw starts moving from side to side and you can't even hold a sentence with someone. You know you want to go to Soho and take your frustration out on a hooker that you can't even get hard for or you get thrown out for taking too long.

You have sniffed so much that your heart starts racing so fast, you can actually hear it beating and you're so paranoid even your mind plays games and starts to scare you. You're sat there sweating and feeling agitated, listening to every noise and creak, waiting for those that are not even there to come and get you. While, also checking your pockets five, maybe six times for nothing and looking at every call made on your phone.

The never-ending feeling that you're looking for something but can't find it, going over the numbers in your phone twenty times, feeling the effects from the last line you just sniffed. But these effects only come if you have good coke sitting there. Late at night in a state of mind-numbing oblivion from the Peruvian flake. Thinking to yourself in your coked-up trans lucid state that it was indeed your 'precious' sitting upon the mirror.

The Devils Dandruff. Sparkling white cocaine powder waiting for you to indulge in again. Then you pick up the note and start the ritual all over again, wishing the world would swallow you up.

So, that's why the tentacles of the Firm were always there pulling at you to get you deeper involved. It was the whole life style; the Friday feeling of getting wasted. Every time I managed to get away for a little while or back to some sort of normality, it drew me back in. It dragged me away from the normal structure of day-to-day life and the thought that I would soon be able to retire. Retire from the getting, the weighing up and the counting. Sniffing point one of a gram from every gram weighed up. Or the over-mixing, or pressing the testing or being involved with the guns, money and the women.

Having different women around you, not for you, but for what they could get out of you, and not forgetting the strippers, the hotels and the prostitutes in Soho and calling on the escort girls from time to time. Also, those crazy nights with the cocaine binges with acquaintances that after a while would put anyone into a state of psychosis. It seemed my attempt to get out of the Firm the first time had failed, and any hope of me not being addicted to cocaine and women was doomed. I would stay in the realms of the underworld run by villains, gangsters, businessmen, money, power and yes pussy; plenty of pussy.

The women seem to love a bad boy and got as much as they could get for free, and you drank as much as you could drink before you fell over. This would be my life, or else it would be a life behind bars, when they caught me. If something drastic didn't happen. Either that or I would have killed myself from the come downs.

CHAPTER 2

So, getting back to where we were it's like having a line, you mind races of and then comes back again. Just a brief recap so let's rewind back before Mandy had been killed. Dear reader, Mr Nice was now plotting to get a deal sorted with the same Colombian Firm that had ordered the hit men to come over and get me, but in the process, had ended up killing Mandy and taking a van load of mine and Old School's dirty cash.

That was more money than the amount for the long overdue payment I had owed him. The police had caught Mr B and the rest of them with the cocaine and the bank bond that and Old School had got off the Russian Mafia man. He had been Old School's pal from way back from the rave scene, but now he was dead as Johnny had shot him.

At that time, I still owed the Colombian the money for the deal that had gone wrong, which led to six men being banged up and one diver escaping, never to be seen again, which was really strange. One person was badly hurt and two people were dead and I was struggling to pay the Colombians back.

Once, we had the depot money, I thought all my problems would be solved, but that seemed to be the beginning of many more problems, as the Colombian, AKA the Grim Reaper the Columbian Don, already had his hit men looking for me in London. I knew I shouldn't have listened to Old School, that day before we went, who said, 'fuck them you have enough money now pay them when we get back from Spain.'

The Colombian had relationships with the cartel, so when the money that I was supposed to pay him before I went out to Spain was late, bam; he ordered his hit men to come and find me. On their hunt for me they had left a driver the Firm would pay to drive us about in a critical condition. Two doormen wounded from a spray of bullets while they were on the door. Two clubs were shot up. Mandy was shot dead at the hotel and one car was burnt out. They had also kidnapped Mattie the Mac. All this in the process of looking for me to try to collect the money I owed.

After all this, they still got paid and ended up running off with a van load of the stolen depot money that was far more than what I owed the Colombian in the first place. Gutted or what? At the same time Mattie the Mac had bought it on top, for himself and had lost the other van-load of money. Then with the chain of events, he had given the other van that was stashed up to the police. Leaving us with diddly squat.

We thought we still had two vans full of cash stashed up ready to move out to Mr Nice for his mate, the son of an oil billionaire in Dubai, ready for them to clean and make spendable again in other accounts. All for a £1 million pound cut once the stolen money was cleaned. But Mattie the Mac had handed it to the police.

Old School and I didn't know about any of this until we had got back from Mr Nice's place in Spain. We heard about the commotion on the phone and were told that Mandy had been shot. We thought it best we come back sharpish as Mr Nice had said,

"Fellas, I still want my money and I will sort it for you, so get to London to sort this little mess out and then get back out here."

So, we came back to London to see if Mandy was okay. As Johnny the hit man - Mandy's brother - told me to keep looking after her before he went on the run when I had escaped with him from the prison van for the shooting committed out in Spain and in London.

At Dover we escaped Johnny and Mr B by jumping off the prison van. I had intended to look after Mandy like my life depended on it, and now she was gone and had been shot, my life really did depend on it. I was now in danger once again as I was a dead man running in Johnny's eyes.

We had to come back from Spain and we told Mr Nice we had put the money job on hold until we knew what was what! Now we had to risk putting ourselves on offer to the police and try to get Mandy's body back from the old bill before they caught up with Johnny. Luckily for me, Johnny had wound up getting shot by the police anyway, so he really had risked everything. He must have known it was a great risk coming back to England whilst he was on the run. I guess everyone who winds up in this, my world, is a chancer!

Basically, Johnny didn't care anymore as Mandy was all he really had left. Once he knew she was dead, and that I was to blame for her death, all he wanted was me dead too. And who could blame him?

Well, we were back, the money was gone, Mandy was

dead and Johnny had gotten himself killed, so now we had to level with Mr Nice. However, he phoned us and saved us the trouble.

"Hello fellas. Everything is in place?"

That's when I had to say,

"How's your luck Mr Nice? There's no money. It's all gone well wonky, and there's no deal anymore." There was an ominous silence at the other end but in for a penny in for a pound, I had to explain the whole scenario; "There's no money to do any deals with and any money left would be with the Columbians cause they took the van, which I'm sure had a lot more money in it then we owed them. There were three vans, yes? One van that Mattie the Mac got caught with and one the Columbians took and one that Mattie the Mac has given to the police that he has now done a deal with to get less time in side. So, Mr Nice, there's no money, no deal, it's all gone. Every last penny of it and to top it all off, Mandy is dead."

With a booming voice Mr Nice parroted the last word back to me,

"Dead!" One of the most feared and reviled gangsters in London continued, "Johnny is going to cut your head off mate and shove it up your arse and bury you in a suitcase."

"Shit you're kidding me!"

I must admit scary as all this was, it was cathartic to get all this shit off my chest, cool as you like I continued, "Mr Nice, I know I'm a bit of a joker sometimes but here …"

I passed the phone to Old School,

"Mr Nice, It's me Old School, Shit indeed, it's all true mate! Mandy is dead and were working now on sorting things out to get her body back from the old bill if we can and sort a funeral out."

"What about the money?" Mr Nice asked.

The news hit him hard. That's when Old School said they have taken the other van-load and there was more than what we had owed them in there, I'm sure of it, also the police have one also ..."Get the Cookster on the phone."

Even though he had said to give it to them when we were put on the spot by the phone call when I had rang Mattie at the Savoy Hotel, he was still asking for the money.

"How much you reckon Cookster?"

"Probably around 3 million, more or less. It's hard to tell. Once the vans were stashed up and we got them we didn't sit there counting the cash, we just gave a few bundles of it to the fellas that did the job for us. I know one of them was real heavy with money in it."

"So you reckon there could have been two maybe three mill or over?"

"Yes. Mr Nice. But it's all gone now."

"Well, you may as well wipe your mouth with it." Mr Nice continued, "Cookster as it will be in their hands. It's well gone by now and any chance of you and Old School getting it back after the performance with those getting nicked out in Southend, too right it's gone. I think it's highly unlikely you'll ever see them or the money again. You two would do best just to call it a day son and walk away from the Firm. Just think yourself lucky, some things will have to change and change fast. Tell Old School someone will be in touch as normal. A fella called Malcolm. Until then, if I were you I'd keep my head down and my ear to the streets Cookster, and don't let Johnny find out you got his sister killed, and stay away from that old cocaine mate. It twists your mind."

He was being all nice about things, which made a

change, but it didn't sit right somehow. "Well, maybe you could give me their number?" Mr Nice added, "And we could maybe get some cocaine off them. It's always nice to make new contacts in this game, and one like this is hard to come by. So give me the number Cookster."

"The number? I ain't got it Mr Nice. The only person who has it is Mr B. It's his contact."

"Okay Son, look I have other things to sort out now this has happened. You've made me look stupid Cookster running around finding someone to clean the money. So, I'll be in touch with you and Old School soon. I'll set up a meeting with a good friend of mine make sure you go when asked."

Mr Nice was no longer interested in smuggling cocaine! He wanted the money as he himself had put a lot of his own money into a load that was due to come over to London. He knew the outstanding was a lot, and that if he could get out there to the Colombians, then it would be there for the taking. Or would it? As it's not normal to walk into Colombia and demand money from big drug lords, or is it? The usual 'normal' rules simply did not apply to men like Mr Nice.

Anyway, he needed the contact details of the Colombian Don from Mr B, and unless he was going to put himself on offer by returning to London and to visit him in the nick, then he wasn't getting it from him and I don't think Mr B would give it up just like that, unless of course, there was something it for him. So, without it, Mr Nice wouldn't have a chance of marching in there and taking the money back from the depot job. This was the only thing holding him back; the fact that he didn't know the Colombian himself, and the fact he had no contact number to get in touch with him.

Mr Nice was nothing if not a master adapter. Realising Johnny's role as his main man was compromised because of what had occurred in Barbados and with him having escaped from the prison van and being tied in by being wanted by the police, he began making moves to reorganise his hierarchy.

Of course this would be a fortuitous decision what with what would ultimately happen to Johnny. But for now, steps were in place for a geeza called Malcolm to step in as number one, get hold of Mr B's number, filter the shit from the Firm and keep operation Columbia quiet from all of us by meeting us in one location!

This way for him it was money first and cocaine later. It was just money in his hand and he wouldn't have to sell anything to get in front again, making the risk minimal. He knew Old School and I had wiped our mouths with it and with everything going on, we would never have thought of, or attempted to go out to Colombia and try to get the money back for ourselves. Anyway, we now had Johnny to deal with.

Mr Nice had us over a barrel. We had done as we were told. The Columbians were paid so fuck the money; fuck the lot of them. It was one less headache to worry about. Good luck to them. As long as they were not on my back anymore that was okay with me. They had shown they didn't fuck about when it was time to punish someone and would stop at nothing until they got what they wanted.

Mr Nice seemed happy, even if the deal we had set up to get the money over to his pal in Dubai had gone wrong. So, if he was happy, then were we happy too, even if he was out of character. He could have been so mad at us and claim we still owed him for the time he had spent sorting it out, but he knew we were skint and it would be like getting money out of a stone. He knew that we would owe him when he needed us and there was nothing we could say or do.

We had caused all the mess, and anyway, it was Mr Nice who told me to hand the van-load over in the first place. I was on the phone to Mattie to start the moving of the money, but I ended up talking to the hit man. He had called me and said that he wanted to kill me if I couldn't pay him back at the Savoy. If we had stayed back for a bit, I could have paid the Colombian out of the stolen money. Shoulda, woulda, coulda and all that I suppose!

"It could only happen to you two pricks. You two are like the two fucking Ronnie's, you and Old School," he laughed out loud and put the phone down.

Once he had hung up, Mr Nice gave this outstanding money situation a little more thought He needed the contact number of the Columbians Don, Mr Cartel himself, AKA the Colombian Don who runs under the moniker, The Grim Reaper.

The only person now to have a direct contact for him was Mr B, but he was still behind bars doing his time. Mr Nice knew it would be too risky for him to go and see him on a prison visit. After all, they take your photo and prints and he didn't want that. Instead, he would send Malcolm, a good friend he had known since they were kids. They had grown up in the East End and allegedly were known to the jewellery brothers and the horse races. He used to take the bank money that Mr Nice stole way back then, when he was in his early 30's, and put in through the horse races for 'cleaning.'

Unbeknownst to Old School and me all this was going on while we were making arrangements for Mandy's funeral, Mr Nice had been very sneaky indeed about the whole affair. That's why we couldn't work him out. Why he had been so nice. After all, he wasn't the nicest fella in the world when he was angry; hence the ironic title Mr Nice.

Because of all the trouble he had been through to work this deal out, to get the stolen money in to Dubai, you would have thought he would have been a bit pissed off. When we had told him there was no money, he was still so very cool, even though he had spent several grand on us while we were living it up in Spain with him, thinking we were all self-made millionaires during our wait to try and get the money cleaned before we moved it. We were out there in Spain with him working out how to change the stolen money at the time back then and trying to sort out the deal with his Dubai friend.

We had to get the stolen depot money out to the oil rig and then on to Dubai so it could disappear in the oil money before having it turn up in some off-shore account. Then it would be transferred to Wong's account at the exchange right next to his restaurant in London, ready to use and as clean as a whistle.

It should have been in there like most times, ready for them to send Wong's minder, the sexy Chinese woman Yan to claim it. Now, talking about Yan, she was something else. I had met her once when I had gone to Wong's place to get some cocaine with the stripper. There was a lot more to Yan than met the eye, I'll tell you more about her and how Wong had met her as we go along.

CHAPTER 3

After I talked to Mr Nice again on the phone back then, what I couldn't understand was why Mr Nice had been so blaze about us messing up the deal with his Arab friend in Dubai; the billionaire son of an oil barren. Mr Nice had gone through a lot of trouble for us to get things sorted with these fellas and it would have cost a bit up front to organise. His mate was the one who was to clean the stolen depot money for us and give Mr Nice a one million pound cut for the introduction and for his time for helping us.

We could not work out why he was so calm about me and Old School running up big debts on his tab in Spain and sniffing large amounts of his cocaine that he had around him at the time, without him wanting or even asking for any payment.

It wasn't in his character to be so cool and easy going about things; certainly not things that had gone wrong and things we had fucked up. In fact, it was a little out of character for him to be over-generous to us and nice. While we were out in Spain it was still okay, but not now we were back and he knew the full story. I guess thinking we were multi-millionaires at the time may have helped us, but why so nice now we were skint?

It didn't make sense. Well, we know the reason now, but more on that one later …

We had found out that Mandy did in fact die from the bullet wound the Colombian men had given her in the Savoy hotel. We then also found out that Mattie the Mac had given up the other van with the stolen cash in it. That's when we knew it had all gone wrong, very wrong, and that I was now a dead man and needed to tell Mr Nice that there was no money.

No excuses, no one to fight my corner. It was just myself and Johnny, who would soon see me sent back to my creator, whoever it may be, now I had joined the dark side. Lucky for me, Johnny was dead before he could get to me.

It was all gone. It had made me a little uncomfortable as it was well out of character for Mr Nice to been so nice about the whole thing. When I had talked to him about it all on the phone, he just said, "Cookster, these things could only happen to you two son," instead of blowing his top or wanting to see me and demanding I still owed him at least half the mill for the fuck up. He had said a few other words but they had gone in one ear and out the other.

Well, the reason Mr Nice was so nice about the whole thing was as soon as I had phoned him and explained what had gone on in London; he knew there was money to be had. If only he could get his hands on it.

After our call he lit up a cigar and thought that he would go out to see the Colombian Don. He walked out onto his balcony and thought, *I'll go get the money back from the van myself*. As he now knew there was far more cash than they should have gotten and if he was going to lose one million with us for cleaning it, then he was going to make sure he was going to get two million for getting it back. Even if it meant getting it back from the Colombian himself. What did he have to lose by going over and asking for it back?

His life.

Nothing to lose and he knew it.

Now Mr Nice desperately needed the contact number for the Colombian Don, and the only person who had that was Mr B. So Mr Nice had Malcolm go to see Mr B inside Spring Hill Prison to get a contact number from him for the Colombian drug Baron, so that Mr Nice could get out there and see the Colombian drug baron, AKA the Grim Reaper as he was known to us at the time. Malcolm was told by Mr Nice to tell Mr B he needed the contact number.

"So, why does he want it and what do I get? This is worth a lot of money in the right hands Malcolm."

Malcolm was told to say that Mr Nice was looking at trying to have a go at a major cocaine smuggling deal to make up for what he had lost in France. That now that the French job had been messed up, he wanted to pull his own one off and be in control of the whole lot, as there were still a few people out of pocket.

"He said to say that if you gave the contact number over he would bring you in on it once you're released from prison," Malcolm said. Mr B only had a year to go and if he got parole he could be out. "If you give us the Colombian contact, then he would look after you financially, with a lump sum when you're released. He promised he would set you up again. He said he would put money aside for you from the deals that would take place. But he can't set up the deals without the contact."

Mr B agreed and in return for this info, gave the contact number up without knowing that Mr Nice was in fact bluffing and had no intention of getting the cocaine back. He just wanted the outstanding money. Mr B had no choice but to believe in it. Otherwise it meant that Mr B would be released from prison with nothing, as the police had taken everything from him; house, cars, etc. So he had no choice with an offer like this put to him while he was stuck inside. So he coughed up.

"Here, think you'll remember it?"

"Yes. Well, got to go. If you can make a friendly call as well if poss so he knows he will be calling."

"Will do."

Once Malcolm had passed on the number Mr Nice arranged to go out to Colombia and talk business with the Grim Reaper. Mr Nice had contacted him and he had explained who he was and how he knew Mr B. Mr B had confirmed that he was a friend, and yes business could be done if Mr nice came out to Colombia to see him first. Mr Nice had agreed it was best for him to come out and talk face to face mano a mano.

"I want to talk to you about a two million pound deal."

"In that case," replied the Colombian drug baron, "I look forward to seeing you and you can see how things work here."

The deal Mr Nice wanted wasn't for cocaine, like he had now managed to let everyone believe, even the Columbian Don thought that when he had called he was coming out for the money if the done had none he would have told him not to bother and may have put a hit man on to him for taking the piss.

Even Malcolm really thought that it was for a Cocaine

deal adn not about getting the stolen money back. Mr Nice thought if he got it back he could take the two million back to Spain and get ready for his friend in Dubai, the oil owner's son, to sort it out and get it ready for him to use all clean. Back to plan and some!

Or, he could transfer it, little bits at a time as and when he needed it, through Wong in China Town at the exchange next to his restaurant.

CHAPTER 4

Mr Nice then spoke to the Colombian and told him he was a good friend of Mr B's and that he was now banged up, and that he had wanted him to get in contact with him to talk some business. The Colombian had said,

"No disrespect, but give me your number and I'll be in touch with you, as at present I don't know you from Adam."

Once the Colombian had checked him out, he rang Mr Nice and Mr Nice said he wanted to do a big deal. About two million's worth, which was a deal the Colombian couldn't refuse. So the Colombian invited him out there to talk business; to discuss who was going to arrange the transportation of such a large consignment and how payments were going to be made etc. To do it by phone would be too risky and the police authorities would be able to track their whereabouts by the phone and there calls, so the Colombian told him to come out and see him face to face to make arrangements. He wasn't coming to Spain or England in a hurry, so if Mr Nice was serious, it would be best if he flew out to Colombia for the discussion. *Talk was cheap but actions spoke volumes*, he said.

Mr Nice knew he wasn't going out there for the Cocaine and that it was just to get the outstanding stolen money back from the robbery that they had taken from the van. But the news of a large deal going down with the Colombians with a large amount of Cocaine coming over soon meant Malcolm and the other Firm members were now running around him once again. Thinking soon they would be working and sorting out the Cocaine once it arrived in England. They thought that it was a genuine trip to organise some Cocaine to come over. Even Mr B thought that, as the last thing Malcolm had said to Mr B on his visit when he had handed the number over was,

"Don't worry Mr B. You know Mr Nice will take care of you for this when you get out once the cocaine comes over."

Mr Nice now knew he would get two million pounds and he knew he wouldn't have to tell anyone about it. It was a sneaky move, but hey, if you could get away with it and you were him, wouldn't you have done the same thing? Mr Nice thought that after all, he was the one calling the shots.

This was kinda payback time for our messing up. It's amazing when people think you have loads of money or Cocaine. They're your best friends in the world. When they realise you don't, they don't even call you to ask how you are. When you're making money for the Firm they treat you like this;

"Hello my friend, come eat and drink and sniff and shag as much as you want with us."

But once you owe them money it's a whole different story, more like this;

"Find him, get him, hurt him and kill him. Add more money to his bill." Nothing more than, "Where's my money? Don't call me till you have it." Or even like this, "Once I find you, you best have it. See you in a week's time unless they get to you first." So, Mr Nice was now on his way out to see the Colombian drugs baron.

CHAPTER 5

When he arrived, Mr Nice was greeted at the airport by a
blacked-out people carrier, courtesy of the Colombian drug
baron. He was then driven at speed to the meeting place,
which was in an isolated apartment, away from the main
town and near where the old people lived where cocaine
was their life.

The drug baron wasn't there so Mr Nice was met at the
apartment by friends of the Colombian's. He was told to
empty his pockets, which he did. He was then searched and
patted down as he looked around at his surroundings. He
saw what looked like a women sitting in a chair facing away
from them. The man that had patted him was now checking
inside his belt line and under his leg at the bottom of his
trousers. He was then told to turn around.

"Look, I'm clean. Why would I come armed?"

He was told to turn around again and he was searched
from the back as well. Then the man searching him said to
the women in the chair, "He's clean."

The woman stood from the chair and walked over to
him. She was the Colombian drug baron's daughter. Her

name was Maria, she was petite with long black hair with a gorgeous smile but she wasn't smiling now. She was about 26 with tanned skin and was wearing jeans and a white t-shirt which hugged her fair sized cleavage. Small beads of sweat were visible on her forehead from the heat. She walked around Mr Nice looking closely at him, telling him to unbutton his shirt while the fan above buzzed, letting off some much needed cool air.

"Sorry?"

"Just do it. You won't like me when I'm angry."

She wanted to see if he had any recording devices. She then put a gun to him. "Do as you're told, open your shirt," she demanded.

He slowly unbuttoned his shirt, revealing his chest. Satisfied, she lowered the gun.

"Okay," she said, "drop your trousers."

"What?"

"Do it." Mr Nice knew that she wasn't messing around as the other men with her were looking at him in a mean menacing way. He did as he was asked and realised he was a little out of his depth.

Maria added, "Pants." He did as he was told and she then told him to get dressed knowing now he was completely clean from everything.

"Let's go."

Mr Nice was then ushered back into the car as they all got in. Mr Nice finished doing his shirt up and put his jacket back on. They were then driven back in to the main town to the Colombian's house. As he got out, he saw the splendour of the very plush-looking house. It had four modest looking cars parked outside, and a nice Audi. The house had its own working staff inside and two big Rottweiler's guarding the grounds. The Colombian drug baron wasn't there either. He was away on more important business. Now, in better light and knowing who she was, Mr Nice was wowed by Maria's good looks.

"So, Mr Nice. I take it you were expecting to see my father. He has been telling me all about you and your visit to us to arrange some business," she smiled. "He tells me you're this big-time gangster from London that now lives in Spain with two million to spend."

"Yes, well you could say that, but not too loudly." She laughed,

"Don't worry, you are amongst friends out here."

Maria explained that Mr Nice was welcome to stay at the house instead of a hotel. Her thinking was she could keep a closer eye on him until the Colombian drug baron got back and that there would be no need to book a hotel as to stay at the house would mean less people would know he was out there.

He was helped with his bag by the minder. He wasn't planning on staying longer than five days. His intention was to get the money, go back to Spain and buy himself a nice villa in Marbella!

The Colombian drug lord would be back to meet Mr Nice in a few days. He had been dealing with some property matters and papers that had been drawn up. They now wanted the Colombian drug baron's signature on the paperwork, so he had to stay in Cuba. He had unfortunately overlooked this as he thought he would be back in time to meet Mr Nice.

"My father thought he would be back in time to meet you, but he is waiting on some paperwork that requires his signature. Something to do with some hotel developments that he wants to buy in to, or is buying off a Cuban at a cut prices. They owe the family some money and the only way they can pay him back and stop the paper trail is by doing this property deal."

"Nice house you have here."

"Glad you like it. It will all be mine one day."

Mr Nice looked at her and again and thought how beautiful she was as she asked him if he would like a drink

She poured one for them both and they sat down close to each other.

"So, tell me about London, as I haven't been there yet."

After talking for ages, it was as if they had known each other for a long time. Mr Nice unpacked. He could tell she liked him and the feeling was mutual. She was kind of quiet. She took him out in to the bars and clubs and they hit it off in a big way. They had a few drinks and a few lines. They didn't get back until the early hours of the morning.

Once they had left the last club, on the way back to the car, they started kissing and caressing each other, until they were soon tugging at each other's clothes. She liked her Cocaine, as we all did back then. She was sniffing it like her life depended on it. He knew then she had some sort of Cocaine problem. Fuck me, half the Firm did and Peru and Columbia definitely did, but it seemed only a few of them could keep it under control, while the others struggled to contain it.

I guess having a Dad as a Colombian drug baron, and having her family being connected to the Cartel wasn't helping her cocaine habit one bit. In fact, it probably caused it. When most kids were enjoying lollies and sweets, she was hitting the Devils Dandruff in a big way. As it was on tap day and night, without having someone to foot the bill.

Somewhere down the line, Mr Nice had taken her down to the beach and they started to make love. She slipped down her knickers and fumbled with his jeans. They had wild sex right there, on the sand, in the moonlight. The Sea lapped at the beach and the moonlight shone off their gyrating bodies. He let her slip off and they lay there, coked up, looking at the stars. It was very passionate. They adjusted their clothes and she drove them home. Once back at the Colombian Don's house, she took him into her bed and they cuddled up and made love again. Yes indeed this was proving to be a very stimulating trip.

CHAPTER 6

Eventually the Grim Reaper himself came back to meet Mr Nice just as he said he would. The Colombian drug baron had asked his driver to take Mr Nice to the cocaine field to meet him just as he was landing there. Mr Nice was driven into the jungle, and then they walked on until they got to the field. The Colombian drug baron was there with a minder and he walked over and greeted Mr Nice.

"My friend! Glad you could make it."

"Hi. Nice to finally meet you too, and thanks for letting me come over to speak to you personally like this at such short notice."

"A contact of Mr B's is always welcome. Just so you know, I wouldn't let just anyone come over here Mr Nice, you do understand this? I have asked you here as a sign of respect as I know what you're all about and I also know that you are a major player in England. You're on the lips of most Firms so this visit will work out quite well for the both of us Mr Nice, I'm sure."

"Okay."

"Cocaine? If this is what you want Mr Nice then take

a look around you. You have come to the right place. This is the mother-load my friend, as you can see." He said gesturing grandly at acres and acres of cocaine plantations, he continued, "I am handing this field to my daughter as I'm getting a little old for all this stuff. There is a lot going on here. A lot of cocaine will be coming and going from this field very soon. I have given this to my daughter to take care of. It has already served its purpose to me and the Cartel, but I don't think she can do it alone. I already know she has a problem with cocaine and I can't be here babysitting her every move. I have other business matters to work on, and to be here looking after the field, or should I say overseeing it. I will give you cocaine by the tonne, if you can shift that amount. So do we have a deal?"

There was no bull shit preamble with this level of player, the Grim Reaper continued, "Also, for every key I get across for you I want one hundred American dollars extra. Unless you have the means to do it yourself? Then it will be a one-off price that we can agree on. But let me tell you, be too greedy and you are a dead man."

"Yes, understood."

"Then we have a deal. I know you have some very good connections in Ireland, Germany and also England, which is good. I hear you have good contacts in Liverpool, where I'm also very accustomed to. Also, people tell me that you're also connected to a main contact in Amsterdam and Sicily. I hear your tentacles are now also reaching out to the Russians, which I like very much as the Cartel has business with them too. Whether that's true or not it doesn't matter to me."

He added in grave tones, "What does matter to me Mr Nice, is my family, my money and my daughter's future. The field is her future for now. Until it has made her a comfortable living. Just as I and others have had the pleasure of enjoying for these last few years. What I like about you is that you come very recommended and trusted. I hear you have worked with the best and that you run your own smuggling operation, and are nearly at the top of your game. The only thing letting you down as far as I can see is that you have to pay someone for your cocaine before it comes to you."

"Yes."

"Ha ha, Mr Nice, that's the difference between being in control of the biggest drug Cartel in Europe and thinking you're in control. So how would you like to be at the very top of your game and not have to pay anyone? He asked raising an eyebrow. He took a step closer to Mr Nice and raising his arm continued. "Let them be the ones paying you. Then you really will be the man who runs the biggest drug-smuggling operation. You'll become a kingpin my friend. Think about that. I know a man with a lot of contacts. He is a very trusted man, and can have a lot of say with regards to the drugs trade. Not many people get to make the contacts you seem to have been able to enjoy along your way, my friend. Not many people make it this far." (And nor would Mr Nice had, if he hadn't had Johnny as his trigger man.)

There was a little uncomfortable silence and then the drug baron continued, "They're either dead, drugged up in the gutter somewhere, or in prison."

"Look, I'm not here for cocaine,"

"What?" He asked The Colombian, surprised as hell. "Wasn't that what we talked about before I asked you out here?"

He stopped walking and turned to face Mr Nice full on his new body language said it all.

"Mr Nice, if you're not here for cocaine then it seems you're in the wrong place." He pulled out a revolver. "What do you want? And why have you come here?"

"I'm here for the money that was taken by your hit men. From the van in England."

"Money, Mr Nice?"

"Money that the Cookster owed you for the deal that had gone wrong in Southend with Mr B. With the shipment you sent over for him. You know the van that was taken by your men for payment for that debt he owed. There was money outstanding in the back of the van and that's what I have come to take back."

"I have never heard of this Cookster man. This man you're referring to, the young fella about twenty-nine that I met in Stringfellows with Mr B? You mean the gangster's runner by any chance? As he told me that he was known as. Not the Cookster."

"Well, yes. They're two and one of the same. They're the same person."

"And, Mr Nice?"

"Well I'm here to take it back."

"Ha ha." The minder punched Mr Nice in the stomach and caused him to fall to his knees. The Colombian kicked him down to the floor. He then put the gun away.

"Take it back Mr Nice? I don't think so," He said waving his arms around. "Look around you. Does this look like the place people just come to and take things back from me? Ha ha."

Mr Nice looked around him and saw that there were about four armed gunmen. All of whom were holding automatic weapons. He lay there in the dust holding his stomach. The minder forced him to stand up again.

"No. I just want what's outstanding from the debt." He wiped the dust from his clothes.

"Mr Nice, we all want things in this life but we don't always get them."

That's why the Colombian drug baron had brought him out here to the cocaine field for the meeting. So, if things went wrong, he could just finish Mr Nice off and no one out here would care. Life was cheap out here. He knew he would be protected by his own gunmen. They were employed to look out for the security of the cocaine field and the drug baron.

"Ask for it, maybe Mr Nice, but not take, my friend." Mr Nice turned back and looked at him again, knowing that in fact he was out of his league here and that Johnny was no longer watching his back. He wasn't sure of his future now. He now knew he had taken a risk coming here alone, as he hadn't really thought this one through.

"I had you checked out the minute you got off the phone to me. Although Mr B passed my number to you, it doesn't mean you can come out here and take what you want. I like to surround myself with a certain calibre of men. Not liars and cheats. It seems you have lied to get out here. I know your capabilities. I also know about the work your friend Johnny does for you. Yet you come here alone, which puzzles me, but which I also like and respect. It's my business to know these things. I know where you live, breath, sleep and shit Mr Nice. I also know that you run a major operation with the exportation of large amounts of Ecstasy and Cannabis, which to me has been of very little interest. I thought I would bring you out here so you could see for yourself how things work this side of the water. Asking me for the money like that takes a lot of balls and has made me laugh."

He went on … "That money is gone and is now buried in a very safe place Mr Nice. If you ask me again for the money, you will be gone and buried in a very safe place too. But unfortunately for you it may not be so nice. Have I made my position clear to you? I'm the lion of this jungle. Just as you may be the lion of your jungle. Right now you're standing on my territory and I'm doing all the roaring. Do you understand me Mr Nice?"

Then the Colombian's daughter jumped out of her jeep and came running over.

"Father!"

"Hi. This is my daughter." He said and turned and smiled at her. "I'm sure you two have already been acquainted. In more ways than one, so I'm told."

He already knew what had been going on. The butler that had driven him to the field had talked to the drug baron on the phone earlier, before he had landed in the field. Also, the Colombian's guard team had followed Mr Nice as soon as he had landed, and they had been watching him the whole night.

"Yes, we have already met," Mr Nice said.

"Good, that makes things a lot easier for me then."

The drug baron could see the attraction between his daughter and Mr Nice already, even though there was an age gap between them. But he liked this as sometimes with age comes maturity, and he knew Mr Nice was very mature and could teach his daughter a great deal about this business without even trying.

He also knew that he was a major link to England's underworld. He thought he would be smart regarding the business, as he knew his daughter couldn't look after such a responsibility on her own, not just yet. Even though she was twenty-six, it was still a big responsibility for her. She also had a major cocaine problem. She tried to hide it from her dad as much as she possibly could so he would still give her the field. She wanted to make her own money from the field and not have to keep asking her dad for money and to support her.

"Mr Nice, with regards to the money my men took off this Cookster, as you now call him, let's forget all about that. It has been paid to a Russian friend of mine as we are working on a submarine, and if you ask for it again then you leave me no option but to get rid of you. You know, my men will take you out of the game in no time. The money is gone! There is no change left I'm afraid."

He paused, a total master of his universe, "What I'm prepared to do for you, as I see you two have already become acquainted, is this; I will give you a share in my field, if you help my daughter look after it. You can take control of it, be your own boss Mr Nice, without having to pay someone for the cocaine before it lands in your hands and gets passed on to your contacts."

He smiled, negotiating was easy when you had this level of control.

I am a generous man Mr nice, working like this you will make quadruple the amount, once it hits the streets of London, or wherever else you're able to get take it. This is the top of the ladder Mr Nice. Now you can either sit at the top of the ladder, or fall off the ladder and be eaten by the snakes. There are a lot of those in this business as you yourself already know. My friend, the choice is yours. Dead or alive, it's no problem for me. To me it doesn't matter as there are many of you in this world that are trying to climb the same ladder, but they will not succeed. I'm handing it to you on a plate."

Again he smiled, cherishing that familiar feeling of holding all the cards, "This is all I have for you. Otherwise you can go back to whatever place you came from empty-handed, or, this may be the last time you see daylight. It's down to you. There's no money here until you earn it."

He closed his eyes menacingly, "I will be out of the country for a month. I don't need the stress of the field anymore. It has served me well. I'm a little old for all this. Time is moving on for me. This is the best I can do. I will give you a percentage of the cocaine field, but you must stay out here with my daughter and look after it. I take it you are no longer concerned about what I have done with the money from the van that the Cookster, AKA The Gangster's Runner, gave me?"

Sighing a touch whimsically, the Reaper continued, "I'm going to buy some hotels out in Cuba and retire. I'm leaving the field behind and building a great future for my family. Once the sub is done then I can relax and let others take the risk, and I will still get paid. If you don't accept my offer, then you need to get on the plane back to where you came from while you still can. As you know, I run the biggest, most sophisticated organisation out here. That's why people like you don't just take, and if they do take it's on my terms and conditions otherwise I will have you chopped up and put in a suit case. If they do take from me they have to make sure they put it back from where it came from, and that's my pocket. Otherwise, I put them back to where they came from. You understand Mr Nice; this is business, nothing personal."

Mr Nice looked at the Colombian drug baron and then at his daughter. He thought for a second as the minder glared at him, cocking the shooter.

"Well, Mr Nice?"

Maria smiled again. *Fuck it*, Mr Nice figured. *Decision made.*

"Okay, I'll move out here and stay with Maria. I'll keep an eye on the field for you for the month until you work out your business arrangements. Then we'll talk again. What percentage will you give me?"

"I will give you a ten per cent share from every tonne that leaves the field and gets sold to Miami. Once we know how much you need to go to England, then we can talk business on that."

"Okay, you have a deal."

Mr Nice shook the Colombian Don's hand. He knew it was worth much more than the stolen money that had been in the van from the depot heist. Two loads of cocaine moved from the field would have made near four million at every harvest. Mr Nice would now be quid's in. This was the place were money came before bullets. Out here every man was made equal by the Smith and Weston, and sometimes people died before questions got answered. People looked the other way when bribed with the right amount out here.

As Alan F had once said when we had sat at the table after all this was going on in the club that night when we meet Malcolm for the first time. He was chatting to Carly K, 'Columbia … This is where money grows on trees!"

This was it. Mr Nice was now in with the Cartel; he was at the top of the ladder. The Colombian had also told him that he had a pilot that would fly cocaine over for them. They had a plane. The Colombian Don showed him where the landing point was and where the plane was kept. It just circled enough to come in and land without being spotted. It re-fuelled and loaded up just a few miles behind an airport.

"Here, Mr Nice." The Colombian said as he handed Mr Nice a fat Cuban cigar to welcome him to the family. "So we have a deal then?"

"Yes," Mr Nice said, more than happy with himself as he had well and truly landed on his feet. He was well in with the family and was now at the top of his game. Maria was ecstatic and rushing over she kissed and cuddled her dad, and then Mr Nice.

"Welcome to Colombia. I must go now. I have other matters to deal with."

He then went back to a field next to the cocaine field, got into the waiting helicopter and left. Reacting quickly to how the scenario had evolved, Mr Nice phoned Malcolm and told him to get a deal sorted with the Liverpool mob ASAP! The Liverpool mob were the ones I had met that time when I had driven the Japanese car down for them. They were interested in fifteen kilos of cocaine.

Within four days the Colombian Don's pilot arrived. He was the short burly type with a bushy moustache and forearms like fucking Thor. His name was Norberto and he been on The Grim Reaper's pay roll for nearly 30 years.

"I'm ready to work. Once the cocaine is ready we can fly it out."

"Okay," said Mr Nice.

Malcolm came out to see Mr Nice. They were taken across the lake to an old aircraft hangar where the light aircraft was parked, well out of sight of prying eyes. Unless you knew it was there you wouldn't notice it ... Malcolm had a meeting with them over in Ibiza and they had confirmed that they would take twenty kilos if we could get it over to England. We needed to get it ready for the Liverpool mob who were eagerly waiting for it.

"Look, get them to take the twenty, pay for the ten, and then pay the other ten within a few weeks or so once we get it to them," Mr Nice said.

Malcolm had a chat with them and the Liverpool mob had then confirmed it with him.

"Yes, get it over and we'll play with it and get the money sorted."

Malcolm then told Mr Nice that they would definitely take twenty, and they had already given the money for ten up front so they needed to get it over there.

"I'm working on it Malcolm. I'll get the pilot on his way soon."

Now that money had changed hands, the deal was set. All Mr Nice had to do was get the twenty kilos over and business would start once again. We had worked with the Liverpool mob before, as I had met them at Knightsbridge the time I also met Stella who owned the jewellery place in Oxford Street.

She was the one I was shagging till we robbed her and she went on to get married. So there was none of this cash on delivery thing going on as they had already just paid for a shipment of puff that had gone over to them from Spain. They were now waiting for the next lot to get organised. Mr Nice and Malcolm were now working out the next lot of puff to come over on the lorry, but that was all in good time. There were more important things to deal with right now. Cocaine was the currency, and they were out there getting it all ready.

So, Mr Nice had told the pilot to get the light aircraft ready.

"I want you to fly twenty kilos over to England and get them to drop it off in our mate's farm field. Can it be done?"

"Yes it can, but it will mean lots of stops for re-fuelling."

"Do you know the places you will be able to do this without getting noticed?"

"Yes, but it will cost every time I land and I will need this to make sure things run smoothly." He pulled out a revolver. "You never know when you land at these places what might happen." He tucked the revolver away in his jacket. "Pay me first."

Norberto continued, "Pay me and then I will do it."

Mr Nice wasn't sure about this.

Mr Nice arranged for half payment to be brought to him, which Malcolm did, and while they did the deal Malcolm also managed to steal the gun.

"Get it over and then we will talk about the rest of the payment," said Mr Nice.

"Okay."

"Okay let's do it then."

CHAPTER 7

The plan was set and Norberto and Malcolm were ready and waiting for the cocaine to come to them at the hanger. Once on board they would then fly to the place and Malcolm would be waiting for it in the field where the drop off point was set. His role would be to fly with Norberto and then go on ahead of him ready for the drop. Malcolm had a good relationship with the owner of the field who had agreed to let the parcel be dropped there, ready for Malcolm to pick up.

This farmer they knew was also letting Mr Nice's contacts use one of the barns at the farm to knock up base speed amphetamines. Once they made it, it would then be driven up to Oxford and stored in two big freezers out on an allotment in a big shed.

The shed was certainly proving a God send as Wong was also using it occasionally to store fake DVDs for the Asian Firm he knew well and more tentacles abound cos those dudes were 'in' with the Russians. The Russians were helping to bring immigrants in from Vietnam, yet again to flood a new market demand!

But, as is so often the case, things were running from

the smooth course as the Asian Firm that was using his money for this organised crime had been nicked, leaving Wong with loads of copied DVDs! So, he had gotten some Chinese women to come down to London to sell them on anywhere she could; in warehouses, markets, pubs and anywhere these guys could go to shift the shady stuff! Ho-hum, never a dull moment, I tell ya!

CHAPTER 8

The processing plant in Colombia now had a tonne of cocaine leaves ready to turn them in to paste and baked into blocks ready to be moved. Mr Nice had recruited a load of eager young boys of fourteen and fifteen to help him sort the cocaine out and put it through the process with the help of one of the older fellas. Man, we are talking some kinda Victorian Mill Owners wet dream with this kinda operation!

He wanted the first lot of cocaine to be loaded onto the back of the truck, ready to be driven to the first pick-up point. There, they would drop the sixty kilos to be sailed over on a sailing boat to the contact in Miami. They would then drop the sixty kilos off at the drop-point and they would then take the other twenty on to the pilot, ready to fly it over for them to England as arranged.

So, sixty for the drop and twenty for Mr Nice, which made eighty kilos that had been made up and loaded onto the old truck, ready to be driven as and when. It was all in big green sacks ready for the rendez vous with Malcolm.

Once the truck was loaded, Mr Nice got in with the two lads waiting to take it to the drop points. Mr Nice and the boys drove off out past the guards of the cocaine field. They had got about half a mile out towards the first drop point when they heard gun shots going off in the distance. The shots came from the general direction of the cocaine field. They also saw a few explosions going off.

Mr Nice put his foot down as the two farmer boys started shouting at him in Spanish told him where to drive and to come off the track. They shouted not to go by the main route or to the main drop-point. So, they pulled off the main track and then went down a back route, which was a rough drive through the undergrowth. It would have been too risky to go the normal way.

Mr Nice pulled off the track and came to a river just as there was another big blast and a cloud of black smoke coming from the same direction. The cloud from the first blast could be seen by everyone, high in the sky. It was obvious that something had been blown up. Then followed another, smaller blast. The lake was well off the track to the original drop-point. The boys told Mr Nice to help them unload the cocaine into a little river boat that was stashed nicely hidden underneath the brambles and undergrowth.

Once the boat was loaded, there was only room for Mr Nice to squeeze in with no rowers. The boys got jumped the water and swam, pushing the overloaded boat and Mr Nice out into the river, leaving the jeep behind.

The current helped them and took them about two miles downriver from the field, and about five miles away from the main airport runway strip where the pilot and Malcolm were waiting.

If it wasn't for the boys, they would have got caught. Man, their instincts were sharp and in this odd context, the desperate little bastards were fucking heroes!

On the back strip of what was loosely considered the run way, there was swampland and marshes just outside the perimeter. Mr Nice asked the boys where they were going and they said they were taking him the back way to the old shack where the pilot kept his plane.

That was where Malcolm was waiting with the pilot. They said it would be safer this way as they knew there was an old deserted shack next to it. No one ever went there and they used it to sleep in sometimes. They could stash the rest of the gear there until things were okay again and then they could move it.

Mr Nice was panicking a little. He knew it had been a close one when he saw the old looking shack and the aircraft hangar next to it. He knew they were safe, as now it was on a little bit of land with one of these tin huts. The boys were heading there as they knew it was desolate and out in the middle of nowhere and only a little way away from the pilot and Malcolm.

But Mr Nice did not feel good, his old instincts were kicking in and he was conscious that this was new turf for him, a whole different environment and he wasn't getting any younger. Yeah no shit, this veteran was nervous as hell!

They all got out of the water, covered the cocaine with the boat and walked over to the shack. It was the epitome of desolation. Literally, the ideal place to stash the cocaine safely until things calmed down, or at least until they found out what had happened back at the cocaine field. Everyone on point, they returned to the boat to secure their coke!

Mr Nice was putting those big ole tentacles out. He was simultaneously sorting out a puff smuggling deal over in Spain, where as you know the old boy had great connections. The plan ran like this: they would get the puff sorted out on the lorries before the pilot could then fly on his own to England with twenty kilos of cocaine on board, ready for the drop in the farm field.

But back in Columbia, eventually Mr Nice and his boys had the eighty keys all stashed in the shack, Mr Nice and the boys started to have a look around thinking what they were to do with it next. Mr Nice's nerves were easing though, everything felt reasonably safe for a moment.

At the pilot's place they met up with Malcolm and Norberto so they could lay low for a bit.

"What's up Mr Nice? You look a little stressed."

"Look, Malcolm, between you, me and the boys, I think it's come on top. The boys said they heard gunfire and I saw the clouds of smoke from the cocaine fields as we left but we stashed the cocaine over there, so it's safe."

"Okay," the pilot said, "quickly then, lets load the plane and get the fuck out of here."

Cautiously, they went over to where the cocaine was. Mr Nice pulled back the canvas sheet that was covering it. Malcolm's eyes widened at the sight.

"Shit! Thought it was only going to be twenty, not eighty!"

"Yes, shit indeed. Now load twenty keys."

"Let's get the lot on."

"No, Malcolm it's not mine."

The pilot then interrupted as the boys started putting the keys in the plane.

"I can only carry twenty keys with both of them flying in the plane."

They loaded the twenty keys on to the plane.

Never let it be said that Mr Nice didn't show respect when it was due, that he had no appreciation for others, he snarled,

"Without the boys I would have never have been able to get out of there you know that? We owe it to these boys. Malcolm I'm going back to the Colombians to let them know what's happened and to see what they want me to do with the rest of the cocaine. Here's two grand. Pay the boys to stay here and look after the cocaine and then you two can fly."

"Will do, Mr Nice, and I'll go back."

Mr Nice left the shack and made his way back. Malcolm went around the shack as the pilot started up the plane. He didn't know these Kids for shit and that unsettled him. The cogs started whirring and he thought to himself that if the boys knew the cocaine was there then they could tell the Colombians or anyone where it was. Well, sometimes you just gotta go with the inner voice people; he called them over.

"Come here boys."

The boys turned to Malcolm. Behind the shack Malcolm pulled out his gun and let them have it, right in their head.

Malcolm stared at the pilot.

"What the fuck have you done? They're only kids for fuck's sake!"

Norberto lunged at Malcolm and, as they fought, Norberto was able to wrench the gun out of his hand but Malcolm had been in this scenario before; he swivelled like a ninja, reversed the leverage and broke Norberto's hold of the shooter. In one swift motion Malcolm grabbed the gun and pointed it at his head.

"Look, we don't want them telling the Colombians where it is if we're keeping it,"

"Didn't you hear Mr Nice? It's not ours!"

Still outraged and concerned by Malcolm's erratic behaviour Norberto bellowed, "Shit, why did you do that?

For fuck's sake they were only kids!" Building in rage he added, "Look, if the Colombians think you are trying to rob them then they will kill you."

Cool as ice Malcolm retorted, "We're not robbing them; we are taking what's ours. Mr Nice has gone back to talk to them about it all so move." Motioning with the gun to the plane, at this point Norberto figured that discretion was the better form of valour and so, they both got into the plane.

"Move! Let's go!"

Norberto played with the controls to get them airborne and then started to fly off, ready to refuel nearby and then drop Malcolm off in Spain as planned.

When Malcolm had landed in Spain Mr Nice rang.

"Did you sort the boys out?"

After they had been shot, Malcolm had put the money in his pocket.

"Yeah, they got sorted alright."

"That's great. So they're looking after the cocaine till I come back? That's good."

Mr Nice was now trying to make his way back to Maria to let her know what he thought had happened. But he had got a call from Curtis.

Curtis was Mr Nice's son from a very long time ago, when Mr Nice had been shagging all the strippers after hours. He had got one of them pregnant back in the day. They had split and she had the kid even though Mr nice didn't want him. Well this son of a bitch maybe a real nasty cunt, but I take my hat off to Mr Nice as he had kept in contact with Curtis, but not so much with the mother. He had told her in so many words to jog on, but Curtis was born and he wanted to know his dad;, Curtis always wanted to be part of his dad's life and looked up to him.

The mother had tried to warn him about his father and tried to tell him what he was like and what he was capable of. She had said he was a no good drug dealer, but the boy didn't listen and thought a lot of his dad.

He had looked up to his dad and thrived from the association to his name and he had started to work in the drugs business himself. He was now knocking out the E's in clubs around London that were coming over from Mr Nice's friends in Amsterdam.

Curtis had rung a week ago saying he hadn't seen him for some time or heard from him.

"Well Son, I'm out in Colombia now. Get a flight out here and spend some time with me. Ring me when you get to the airport. You won't need much money; I'll look after you while you're here Okay?"

"Dad I'm here. Come pick me up."

He made a detour and went to meet Curtis at the airport. On the way back from the airport Curtis asked,

"Where are we going Dad?"

Mr Nice had taken Curtis back to the place where the boys were supposed to be hiding with the remaining sixty kilos cocaine. He told Curtis to stay there until he could sort out a hotel for him nearby. Then he could come and do regular checks on the cocaine that was stashed up with the two young Colombian boys, at least as far as he was aware! But when he got out of the car he saw that the boys weren't there.

"Look, Curtis, I need you to keep an eye on this lot," he said as he pulled back the canvas to reveal the sixty keys of cocaine they had stashed there.

"Shit me."

"Yes Curtis, shit me indeed son."

"Is it yours?"

"No, it belongs to some close friends of mine," Mr Nice went on, "I need you to look after it till I know what to do with it or who to take it to."

"Okay."

"I don't know where these boys are mate. They got paid so I guess that's them, but they may turn up. They're only young boys but they work with us, so they're cool if you see them. Anyone else be very careful with, okay?"

Looking at Curtis he always felt a weird mixture of paternal protection and nostalgia for care free wild times, "Okay, look, let's get you a hotel nearby. You have to stay near here and look after this lot for me till I know what's going on and what they want me to do with it."

"Shit dad, are you sure?"

"Look, I don't think anyone comes out here, so it should be cool."

"Dad, with this lot you're looking to get life, if not shot out here. Are you crazy? Mum used to tell me you were well connected but I didn't think you were this connected."

"Just do as you're told Curtis. You know I'll see you right. I always have. I know I haven't been around all the time but you have known why. I have always been there when you needed me though haven't I? Even when you were young. I looked after you even though I wasn't about as much. You know I always will. I always have haven't I? Even when your mum was trying to poison your mind with the silly things she goes on about. Ah, but it's okay when she's spending the money mate remember that one. So, just stay here and look after this lot and make sure those boys are okay if they turn up here."

Mr Nice gave him Columbian Peso's to the value of 400 pounds sterling.

"I have to go see someone about this lot, so wait here. Don't contact me till I contact you okay?" Thinking through important eventualities he added, "Keep your phone switched on. It may take a couple of days but I'll book a hotel nearby so you'll have somewhere to stay. Just every now and then come and check that it's okay here and that it's still here. If you do get caught just say you were going for a walk and you stumbled on it and that's it. No more than that."

"Okay."

"I'm sure you'll be okay out here mate. See you soon."

CHAPTER 9

Just before Mr Nice left Curtis, he received one of those irksome calls, which I guess you could consider, an occupational hazard. The Liverpool Mob had been trying to ring Malcolm, but as he was still flying he didn't answer. This made them panic a little. They had handed over half the money for the cocaine drop and had paid for the next cannabis deal that was coming in on the lorries from Spain. But as Mr Nice had been away and his priority now was this cocaine now.

"Look I told you lot. We'll do this deal within the next few days. I'll then lay the next lot on till it's done. Then you can pay up in full. There's just been a little hiccup our end. It may take a week but it will get sorted, mark my words."

"Calm down, calm down, eh? What seems to be the problem?"

"There are no problems. Malcolm will ring once he has received the drop. So stop flapping and don't call me again on this phone. How many times do I have to tell you lot? Malcolm will deal with it all. You phone his phone and not mine."

"Calm down eh?"

"Don't fucking phone my phone again!"

"Calm down. Our boys will be back from Ibiza soon. They had to go out there 'cause a few of their Firm have just been nicked. It's come right on top for them in San Antonio. Not the main fellas, they're still all good and are all in Liverpool safe and sound awaiting the new drop. So they're staying low till things calm down. They will want stocking up again before they go back out there and I have passed the money on to Malcolm ready for this lot of stuff."

"Look, he will be sorting everything once he's received the drop of the twenty, and the rest will sort out when he arrives in Spain. Make sense?"

"Okay, sound. Will anymore be coming?"

"That's it for now. That will keep you busy for a bit."

"Okay boss. We have given Malcolm half up front and we will pay the other half once we get the parcel, whichever comes in first."

"Well just be patient. We'll be in touch."

"Sound. I had a call from my man yesterday. They have also paid for the first lot of cannabis from the E's they got that were taken out to Ibiza."

"Just make sure everything runs smoothly your end and I'll work on it this end. Malcolm will be back soon and he'll be in touch, ready for the drop. Then everything will run like clockwork as it always does." Always, Mr Nice, come on, if only that were right, frankly this story wouldn't have even been here would it?

Still, this reassurance was all they were seeking, "Sound mate." The phone went dead.

Mr Nice put the phone back in his pocket.

"Once I'm back dad I'll help them out," said Curtis.

"No Curtis. I need you to stay out here in Colombia for now till I know what's what with this lot."

"Well, I could maybe sail some across if you had a boat?"

Mr Nice considered this for a minute, "Now that ain't such a bad idea. But if we put all our eggs in one basket and you got nicked we would lose the lot. Better to lose some of it than all of it."

"Yes you're right. We'll split the parcel up. It's safer that way. Then if things do go wrong maybe we'll get some across at least."

"Well we can't do a thing with it. It's not mine."

"What?"

"Well it's not mine son. It belongs to the Colombians. I'm just looking after it for them till I know what they want me to do with it. I'll be back within a day or two okay? Just look after this lot and stay at the hotel. Make sure you do."

With that Mr Nice left.

CHAPTER 10

Mr Nice had got back and had explained to Maria what had happened to the field - or what he thought may have happened. She then told her father, but Mr Nice hadn't told them about the sixty keys of cocaine just yet.

He definitely didn't mention the fact that he knew that twenty keys were on a flight ready to be dropped off in England. Once it had stopped in Spain, dropped Malcolm off and been refuelled, it would be ready to make the last flight to England to complete the first drop. There's no need to know and you ain't ever gonna know situation and this fell firmly in the latter category!

He had just said that he thought the field had been uncovered and that he had heard gunfire and some big explosions on the way there.

Once the Colombian Don heard the news, he said he would be coming straight back. He told them to stay at the house and not go anywhere else till he got back- just in case. Within a little time, he was back and he was with one of the Cartel.

They drove out to the cocaine field. It was empty and

the place was a mess, still smouldering from the fire that had incinerated the leaves and the residual smell was horrendous. The Cartel man turned to the Colombian baron.

"It seems that the RAFC are responsible for this."

"The Revolutionary Armed Forces of Colombia? They have finally caught up with us."

Mr Nice continued telling his tale,

"These people that came to the field had destroyed it. It was finished. The soldiers had destroyed the field and the processing plantation that was left. They were specialised in coke eradication and just like the drug lords, they weren't messing around when it came to stopping the production of cocaine. The processing plant had been blown to bits. The storage part where the cocaine had been packed and stored had been burnt to a crisp. It smelt of petrol everywhere."

"It seems the field is no good now," said the Don as he walked through the field, looking around.

The Cartel man picked up some empty gun shells off the floor. There must have been a shootout.

"So where's my pilot Mr Nice?"

"How would I know? Can't we replant?"

"Can you smell that Mr Nice?" the Colombian Don asked. "It has also been sprayed with some sort of chemicals and burnt. This field is finished." He sniffed at one or two of the stems of the cocaine plants that were still standing amongst the rest that had been chargrilled.

Beads of sweat were now visible on Mr Nice's head and he also looked a little concerned. Then there was silence as the Cartel man and the Colombian looked at Mr Nice.

"So, now what?"

It was a little uncomfortable for them all.

Then the Colombian drug Baron looked at Mr Nice

and repeated himself.

"So, Mr Nice, where is our pilot?"

"I said I don't know."

"Well then we'd best look."

They drove out to the shack, Mr Nice was now sweating even more and not just because it was fucking humid, but because he found himself in a Jeep with two men holding AK47s sat right next to him. The Colombian Don just sat there staring at him. They looked around and drove down the dusty, bumpy track to where the plane was and to the empty pilot's shack.

"Stop!" Shouted the Colombian Don.

Shit! Mr Nice thought as he noticed that just to the left of them, was the rest of the cocaine stashed and hidden. If they found it, they would have realised Mr Nice was trying to steal their gear. He knew he had to come up with another story as to how it got there, otherwise they would kill him on the spot. He had already lied when he said he was on his way to the field, when he heard all this go down.

They all got out of the Jeep and the Colombian walked straight over to the now empty plane hangar.

"Maybe they have the pilot too?" He walked around and stood next to the canvas where the cocaine was stashed.

Mr Nice hoped his son didn't walk over now and prayed that the Cartel man didn't discover the cocaine under the canvas as he bent down next to it and quickly flicked his fag over there. He stood up and walked away from it but Mr Nice's heart was now beating fast and felt a trickle of sweat rolling down from his armpit onto his body.

As the Cartel man ran over and looked, Mr Nice's heart stopped.

This was it there was no way out of this now. He was a

dead man and he knew it.

The Colombian Don came around.

"It seems they have now got the plane too. And the pilot."

They all walked further into the hangar and saw the two dead boys on the floor. Mr Nice couldn't work it out and was very nervous. He was not sure about his future with regards to the situation he was in. He couldn't think how or why the boys were dead.

The Colombian turned to Mr Nice and glared at him.

"Mr Nice, it seems you have outstayed your welcome. It's time for you to leave my country, but before you leave, I have one question for you. He took hold of one of the AK47's and cocked it, ready to fire at Mr Nice.

This was it. Goodnight Vienna for Mr Nice as he looked at two very dangerous men. Weighing up his options mentally-thinking if he might try to explain that he had saved sixty keys. He thought telling them this may keep him alive.

"Yes?" Mr Nice asked as he started to sweat more profusely and shake a little on the verge of divulging the truth about the sixty kilos ploy. Before he could utter a word, The Columbian Drug baron enquired,

"Where is my cocaine?"

Mr Nice looked the Colombian in the eyes and thought for a second. A bead of sweat trickled down his face. This was it his one chance. The Cartel man threw the end of his cigar to the floor put his foot on it. He raised the gun at Mr Nice.

"Look ..." said Mr Nice, starting to panic.

"Turn around Mr Nice and tell me where my cocaine is."

"As you can see for yourself, it's no good. Burnt. Destroyed. What could I have done?"

"Yet, Mr Nice, it seems they have also taken the plane."

"That one I can't explain."

"So, how did you get away if the others got caught?"

"I wasn't here in the first place. I had gone to the town for breakfast and then when I got here I heard gunfire and came back but laid low for a bit."

"Okay Mr Nice. What about the Jeep we passed on our left at the lake?"

"The boys … They must have …" He paused as he didn't know if they could drive or not and if he got this one wrong the contents of the AK47 would be emptied all over him and he knew it.

"The boys what, Mr Nice?" the Colombian said as the Cartel man took aim.

Mr Nice was lost for words.

"Let me phone the pilot,"

Mr Nice was gobsmacked and knew the end was near. Once the phone was answered and the pilot spoke the Cartel men would let this beast spit bullets of lead into him.

"Let's see what has really gone on."

The plane was rumbling as the phone rang. Glancing down to see a withheld number Norberto ignored the call.

"No answer." The Colombian put the phone down. "Let's go."

The Colombian Don put the phone in his pocket and the Cartel man dropped the aimed AK47 from Mr Nice and told him to turn back around as he gave the gun to the other gunman. Mr Nice sighed with relief. They then both got back into the Jeep and headed back.

Mr Nice's heart was beating faster than ever and he was covered in sweat.

"Mr Nice, it seems for now I have been put out of business." The Don looked at the Cartel man, "it's not a bad thing. It's one less thing I need to worry about. After all it has made me a very wealthy man."

Mr Nice was sweating from the heat and but more so from the situation he was in. Even though it had slightly calmed down, and the situation wasn't so hostile, he knew one false move and he was a dead man. Now he was bluffing about the cocaine that was left from the Colombian. Sixty keys of it.

"You can go back. No need for you to be here now," said the Cartel man "we will book your tickets and you can go home in a day or two."

Mr Nice said goodbye to Maria. They were told by the Cartel man to now sell up, move to Cuba and forget about this life and start a new one otherwise they would be caught.

Soon, the morning came for Mr Nice to be driven to the airport. The butler asked "You ready Mr Nice? Can I have your bags?"

As Mr Nice passed them to him, the Colombian Don spoke.

"I think I will drive you to the airport myself Mr Nice."

They got in the car. Mr Nice cuddled Maria and said it was nice to spend time with her and get to know her. Mr Nice was now a little bit unsure about things.

As they drove Mr Nice said, "Once you get sorted again, ring me and we may be able to do some business together again."

"I may. But like you heard, my business is now in Cuba with the Russians. We are making a submarine and as I told you, will not need anyone outside the circle. You understand Mr Nice. You can never trust some people."

The Colombian Drug baron drove on to the airport. There wasn't a sound on the drive after that last bit of talking until they said their goodbyes.

Mr Nice got out of the car and watched the Colombian drive away before he walked into the airport. . He gave it five minutes, then walked over and changed his tickets. Then he walked out of the airport and made his way to the hotel where Curtis had been waiting for him.

"Fuck me. Two days you said dad! It's been four days! I was worried about you. Is it still there?"

"There's been no sign of any boys and the gear was still there the last time I looked."

"When was the last time you checked?" he asked Curtis.

"I checked early this morning and the cocaine was still there. I just got back. No sign of the boys."

"Don't worry about the boy's son. I know where they are. Well Curtis, for now, I'm the proud owner of sixty keys of Colombian's finest. Twenty are already on their way to Liverpool, and the rest we need to get out of here. Any ideas?"

"Shit dad, like I said, get a boat maybe?"

"Now we really need some help to get this lot out of here. I'll have a chat to Wong see what he can come up with."

The pilot with the twenty keys had now made it to Spain and was refuelling ready to fly on. Malcolm had as planned, got on a normal flight home to London ready for the pilot to come over in the next four days or so. Before leaving, Malcolm handed to Norberto the co-ordinates and map reference for the field where the final stage of the drop was expected.

Meanwhile, Mr Nice called Wong and it was at this stage in proceedings that the police had released Mandy's body so the funeral arrangements could be made!

"Wong, I need a favour. I want you to chat to our German friend for me. Fritz, the man who manages the shipping yard. Take some money out of the exchange and then talk to him. I need him to shift sixty keys of the finest from Colombia for me Wong. Can you speak to him? I need some help mate with this one."

"Okay, I will fly out to Brussels and get talking."

He would need to see some sort of payment first then he could plan it out properly.

He was still a little unsure but a little persuasion and things were okay. Mr Nice had told Wong that he was on his way back to Spain and they should meet to sort out the miner details.

CHAPTER 11

Mr Nice was now back in Spain. He had left Curtis out in Colombia. Wong had organised a meeting with the German and was waiting to get the go ahead from Mr Nice so that he could get something sorted to get it over for them.

The German shipping manager's name was Fritz. He was a middle aged fella who had been connected to Mr Nice who once knew his ex-missus. She used to run a swingers club in Brussels and had introduced Fritz to Mr Nice once when he had come over to Prague back in the day.

He had been asked to look after the security at the swingers' club at the time but he had refused as the money wasn't that great. It seemed to have really taken off over in Prague and they were now doing okay - or was she? As she had now opened a few clubs in Amsterdam as well and that's where she was living now.

Fritz was the one who was also sorting out our puff getting it to Spain for us. Fritz had met a Spanish Firm that worked on the ships and they knew that the Swedish man who owned the yard was too old to take an active role in the day-to-day management. Seeking a quiet life as a Director,

Fritz gladly offered his services as a manager and now through him, they had regular access to boats and ways to transport containers full of gear of all kind across countries. Of course, the Old Swede never knew any shady stuff went down.

They had made plans regarding the outstanding cocaine in Colombia. Fritz initially refused to be involved, he was under scrutiny and was trying to go straight but Wong's minder had her claws into him. With her influence it was agreed for a half cut on the cocaine he would get it to Spain for Mr Nice.

He would then sort things out from there as they had lorries coming and going at all times of the day and night. Perfect for Mr Nice to move whatever he wanted across the border; puff, cocaine, you name it, he moved it ...

Wong then told Mr Nice that the German had said, "Look, leave it with me. I will make sure it gets back here okay. Just leave the money. I'll get it sorted and then I may also have a buyer for it as well."

Mr Nice was now all nice and cosy once again back in Spain and the proud owner of eighty keys of cocaine - six million pounds worth, if not more, once broken down. He was now sitting back, waiting for the first twenty keys to drop in the field promised to the Liverpool Firm. That would once again start getting the money in.

He could then pay Fritz a bit more to bring the rest over. Once the big lot came over money would then once again to be no object for them the street value of 60 kilos of Columbian finest was pushing 50 million pounds and they could push it through the exchange next to Wong's restaurant and then transfer it to Guernsey or Switzerland.

Fritz would arrange a boat to collect both Curtis and

the cocaine that was stashed in Colombia. Then, once it was all back at the shipping yard in Spain, Mr Nice would soon be worth the kind of money most people cannot even comprehend!

Not to mention the large lot of puff they would also get over on two lorries from Spain to England. But that was another deal going down.

It was said, if you had done a line in the eighties, then it would have probably been some of the cocaine that Mr Nice had managed to steal from the Colombians that you would be sniffing. Not that you would care where it came from, as long as it did the job.

With all that had gone down and was still going down, Old School and I were still dealing with things in London.

So, Norberto was then told to fly to England and drop off the twenty keys in to the farm field circled on the map that Malcolm had given him. The map was based on the info that Malcolm had told him about where the drop would be, ready for him to then take it to the Liverpool mob.

Malcolm would then have a rendez vous to collect the Cocaine from the drop and get it ready for the deal with the Liverpool mob. After which it had been agreed that Norberto would fly on to Elstree aerodrome and land. The pilot was told he could stay at a house near the aerodrome that Mr Nice had been renting out to some Vietnamese immigrants, but at the moment, it was vacant.

The Vietnamese fellas living there had been growing their own skunk and had paid Mr Nice a nice back-hander for allowing them to do so, instead of selling DVDs and paying the Triads' money back to them for getting them over here in the first place. Wong had got them selling skunk instead and was taking money off them so the Triads weren't happy at the moment with Wong as Wong said he would pay them as well, but hadn't yet.

The Vietnamese fellas had moved on because inevitably the Triads were looking for them as they hadn't been paid. So, they were moving on to other properties to grow their skunk. This had put Wong in a difficult situation with the Triads not knowing where they had gone. Long and short of it all, this had opened up a convenient little hideaway for the pilot.

It was agreed that the pilot would stay at this house in England, rent free. This way Mr Nice knew exactly where he was by having him at the house in England. He told him he would get his drink once the Liverpool mob had squared the rest of the money with Malcolm!

Once he had got back from delivering it to them in Liverpool at Albert Docks, they would think about maybe him flying back to Colombia to pick up some more cocaine, if Fritz couldn't help out or didn't want to get involved.

On the phone he didn't seem too keen even after he slept with Wong's minder at the first meeting with Mr Nice. Mr Nice was now sure he would do what he wanted once some more readies were pushed his way and with Wong's minder's little persuasion. He knew now there was a lot at risk as the sixty keys were just sitting there with only Curtis checking on them every day. Every day that went by he knew it could be a day the Colombians might discover them or the police over there may bumble into matters!

Mr Nice figured he would tell the German that if he did manage to get this lot over, he would help them get their own lot over if they wanted to and bring them in on a major cannabis deal they had sorted. As well as getting paid a nice drink for helping them. He agreed to help.

Malcolm had also organised the plan with Curtis, as he had come up with the idea of sailing some of the cocaine that was coming over, which wasn't a bad shout. Mr Nice had thought that sending the whole parcel over was risky, because if they did get caught, it would all be gone, so he contemplated on what his son had said and decided to split the cocaine up.

Malcolm had now been introduced to Fritz as Mr Nice had told Wong to get them both tighter to start doing business. Seeing the bigger picture clearly, Mr Nice also said it was high time for the wider Firm to know that Malcolm was now his go to man. He suggested a meeting in London to be arranged so that the Firm could be tidied up and everyone can know that Malcolm was going to be operating as the number one. He believed that Johnny was laying low in Barbados after having escaped from the Prison van back in London.

Now everyone knew who was who and everything could be sorted without Mr Nice having to get too involved himself. He had done enough already.

The gear was still stashed at the old aircraft hangar shack. There was talk that a contact they all knew would take the whole sixty keys once it came over. But these boys shafted themselves as they had got caught on a big fraud scam just before the cocaine could be shifted.

So once again, the sixty keys was still just sitting there for now while they waited on Fritz to put his plan in to action and get it moving across.

There was talk of the Liverpool Firm taking it all, if the family Firm put the money up for them up front, but still there was no agreement or money changing hands as yet, and we were still waiting for the drop. So bottom line, the cocaine was just sat as it had been left. The only cocaine that was coming to England for now would be the initial twenty keys.

Norberto had now set of to England from Spain with the twenty keys on board, flying over the field he thought matched the map and co-ordinates provided he let the parcel drop. Then flew on to Elstree Aerodrome just as he was told to do.

CHAPTER 12

Whilst out ploughing, a farmer had stumbled on a large bale-like parcel. When he saw it there, he inquisitively loaded it onto his tractor. He took it all back to his farmhouse and stashed it up in his stables, ready to investigate. He then contacted his Asian friend from the local town to come and have a look at his find and see what it was. His first thought was that the fly tippers had been in his field again. His friend came over straight away.

"Have a look at this Khan. It just turned up all of a sudden in my field. I'm not sure what it is."

Mr Khan opened the parcel a slightly, just enough to reveal what was inside. He saw the white blocks of powder wrapped up in bubble wrap inside the black plastic bag. Inside them was the wax coating coverings with the Medusa sign stamped moulded on to the wax on the blocks. He pulled the wax back to reveal a very oily block with a shiny fish scales effect along the marble blocks. He pressed his finger into one of the blocks and put it on his gums.

"It's drugs."

"What?"

"Cocaine. This is cocaine. And I'd say a very pure lot as well."

"I best phone the Police get them to come and take it then."

They counted them out and there were twenty of them.

"Look," Mr Khan paused saying, "don't be so quick about things. Do you know how much this lot could be worth?"

"No."

"It's worth erm ... Well this lot here is worth a few bob. Not much mind you, but a fair bit in the correct hands. If you give it to the Police, you'll just get thanks and a handshake and a little article in the local paper, if you're lucky."

"But ... How much is it worth?" the farmer asked curiously.

"Well, it's probably only worth about £30,000 in the right hands."

Mr Khan knew it was worth much more but he had to make the famer believe it was not worth that much at all.

This was music to the farmer's ears. He had just lost some of his cattle to foot and mouth decease and any money he could now recuperate, would come in handy.

"Okay, so who do we go to with this lot then? Who are these right hands that will give us that kind of money?"

"You have to be really careful. This belongs to someone, somewhere and they'll be wanting it back. If you ask the wrong people then you could end up in a lot of trouble. If you want, I'll buy it from you, but we keep this transaction between ourselves."

"Okay, when can I get the money?"

"So, we have a deal then?"

"Yes, take it it's yours. I could do with the money after losing the cattle to foot and mouth."

"Okay," Mr Khan placed the blocks into a potato sack, "I'll take it and be back in two days with the money."

"I really could do with the money now."

"Well, it'll have to stay here then till I get the money to you. I have to see my sons and cousin. I'm sure they will know people that will get rid of this for us."

"Okay then it's all yours. Take it and I'll see you in two days."

True to his word Mr Khan returned with full payment within the two days.

Now he knew what it was, the farmer just wanted it off his farm and the money sorted so he could put all this behind him and move on from it all like nothing happened.

That's all we all want I guess. Smart guy, albeit very naïve. The call had come from the pilot to tell Malcolm that the drop was done. Malcolm was in a café having breakfast at the time.

"Okay, I'm on my way."

He dipped his bread in to the last piece of egg and quickly sipped his coffee. Then he shot out of the café and quickly walked across the road to the car wash. To the Polish washer's amazement, Malcome jumped into his half-cleaned BMW, started it up and drove out of the Polish hand wash garage..

"Here." He thrust a fistful of notes through the open window, "Don't worry about the change."

"But it's not finished."

"I have to go. Out of my way." Malcolm pulled out the car wash quickly.

Malcolm made the call to the Liverpool mob telling them it was now here.

"Give me time and I'll let you know when to send

someone to come down for it."

It was now just a matter of Malcolm collecting it, sorting it out and then distributing it to those that had bought in on it, i.e. get the shit to the Scousers.

It should have been a simple job. Walk in to the field, pick the parcel up, drive back to his flat, sorting it out and then taking it to the people that wanted it or that would be sent down from Liverpool to pick it up.

Unfortunately, in life, in this story, things rarely seem to be as simple as we had envisaged. He got to the drop point and pulled up. He looked into the field with his binoculars to see if he could see it, just like he normally would have on other drops that he had gone on, or on other meets to pick up money, or drugs or guns, whatever the parcel was.

He looked hard, but it wasn't there. He pulled into the farm and spoke to his pal.

"Okay Terry where's the drop?"

"There's been no drop Malcolm. Nothing here mate. The courier has taken five keys of speed up to the allotment in Oxford but nothing else mate, no cocaine has come no plane, nothing. We were also mixing up speed in the barn and then moving it up to an allotment in Oxford ready for Mr Nice to sell on but he said just keep it there for now. Malcolm there's nothing here mate."

"Fuck."

He then phoned Mr Nice.

"Mr Nice it's not here."

"What's not there?"

"The fucking gear. Norberto just rang said it had been dropped and guess what? I'm here with Terry, our farmer, and he's telling me there's nothing. Nothing at all mate."

"Malcolm you gave Norberto the map and co-ordinates right?"

"Yeah. But that doesn't change anything mate. I'm telling you there's nothing here!"

"So, Norberto knows the score, it should be there unless the cheeky bastard has had us over."

"Look, I kid you not," Malcolm interrupted, "It's not here mate. Seems that your pilot has had your pants down Mr Nice."

"Go see him, if it's not there, find out why it isn't and then do what you need to do to make it turn up." So, off Malcolm went.

Malcolm had called Wong who had sent two people there on motorbikes to the house. They knocked on the door Norberto unaware of any of the problems, innocently opened the door and was then bundled back in to the house.

Having forced their way into the house, they shut the door behind them and then one of the bikers went to town on him.

"Move," the first biker kicked Norberto backwards onto the floor.

The poor bastard was being thrown around and beaten up. They were both dressed in black motorbike leather gear with blacked-out helmets on.

"Get the fuck on the floor. On Your hands and knees!"

Confused, dazed and literally battered, Norberto did as he was told. The other one pulled out a gun and held it to Norberto's head.

"Don't move. Move and you know what comes next."

"It's not here. There's nothing here, nothing at all."

The biker holding the gun in his hand, received a phone call which rang with the standard Nokia ring tone.

He passed the gun to the other biker and before he

walked out of the room, he started to remove his helmet giving Norberto a clear look at who was under there. Removing his helmet and placing the phone to his ear. He talks into the phone. "Hello," the man on the line pauses for a second. "It's me, Malcolm and I'm with Wong." Then there was a natural purse.

"How we doing Johnny"

"Look, it's not here."

Malcolm turned to Wong.

"It seems as if your cargo isn't where it should be Malcolm"

"I'll tell them to look again."

"Look again"

"Look, we're here and it's not here. There's nothing here mate."

"Well, if it's not there then you'll have to shoot him in the leg till he tells you where it is."

Malcolm could hear Norberto pleading in the other room from his telephone.

"Look, please! I dropped the gear off."

"Shoot him in the leg." Malcolm shouted. The biker walks back in to the room and is given back the gun. He then shifted aim from Norberto's head to his leg in one swift movement and squeezed the trigger letting of a bang and a flash of light as the bullet fired entered Norberto's leg. Boom.

"Argh!"

"Okay, what's he saying now?" Wong asked.

"Not a lot. Just Argh! What do you want him to say? We'll wait."

Norberto looked at the two bikers and began to plead, "Please, please I did what they wanted me to do. I tell you it's there. I did the drop please. I beg you to look again."

"He's in pain, He still says he dropped it."

"Argh my fucking leg! I dropped it in the field. There's a pylon and an old tractor in the field."

"He keeps saying he dropped it in a field with a tractor and a pylon in it and is now begging us to stop."

"Listen, for every lie he tells you put one in him." Malcolm barked.

The other biker turning to Johnny says, "He's seen you now Johnny, your helmet!"

Putting the phone back into his pocket in the motor bike leathers he then turns and snaps.

"Fuck the helmet. In a few minutes I'll be putting one in his nut if he don't tell me where the cocaine is, so seeing me or not will not matter … He'll be dead!" In a cold menacing movement Johnny turns his attention to Norberto, "For the last time tell us where it is!"

"I don't know! It should be there. Please. I dropped it I tell you. Please, I did what you lot told me to do, so why you doing this to me?" Johnny steps on the wounded leg and places the gun to Norberto's head once more.

"Argh I fucking told you, for fuck's sake. I dropped the gear off," he screamed as he rolled around in pain. "Argh fuck. I dropped the gear! I did! Argh my legs! Shit. I know it was there. It's there I'm telling you. Please there's been some kind of mistake."

Johnny placed the 9 millimetre gun on Norberto's head, as the other biker still wearing the helmet, stepped back a bit.

"There's been a mistake?"

"Yes. A fucking big one. I hate dirty rascals that think they can steal people's gear and get away with it." Johnny started to squeeze the trigger and turned his head at the same time to stop the splatter hitting him. Just then Norberto's phone rang.

Taking Johnny away from the job in hand, he pulled the gun away.

"Go on then, answer it."

"Look, its Malcolm, I know what's happened.

Norberto passed the phone over.

"Don't shoot me. It's for you."

"Don't kill him I think we have made a mistake." Malcolm said. As Malcolm looked over a copy of the map that he had given to Norberto, the realisation hit him that it was possible he may have dropped it in the wrong field.

"Keep him with you. I'm going to check this out as I think he may have dropped it in another field." He then jumped into his BMW and shot to the fields.

Having arrived at the drop point Malcolm looked around. Seeing that the field adjacent to the planned drop of point was the only field for miles around containing a pylon in it was obvious to him that Norberto had been telling the truth. The idiot had dropped it in the wrong place, but I guess shit happens.

"For fuck sake mate, make up your mind. I'm either looking at a dead man or we need to get this man some help as he has a hole in his leg, bleeding all over the place."

"Stop shooting him and get him some fucking help." He then made the call and put Johnny in the picture.

"It must have been dropped, but in the wrong place. Get that bent doc round there and get him fixed up for fuck's sake."

The phone went dead.

Johnny turned to the other biker and shouted, "Quick wrap the leg up to stop the bleeding."

Norberto breathes deeply, realising that his situation has improved he sarcastically says,

"Oh so you want to be my friend now eh?"

"Shut the fuck up or you will still get one in your nut."

The other biker took off her helmet to reveal her long hair. It was Wong's minder, the beautiful Chinese woman who had nearly beaten the Norberto to a pulp.

Yang, Wong's minder made a call to the doctor who the Firm were scoring Vida cane from to mix and press their cocaine with. Yang told him to come round to sort the Pedro out.

Within time there was a knock at the window. It was the doctor.

"What can I do for you this time?"

Yang walked the doctor into the room where Pedro was bleeding on the floor with the two bullet holes in his leg and Johnny pressing down trying to stop the blood flow.

"Sort him out will you?"

Malcolm then came round to the place where they all were and tried to establish exactly what had happened. On the drive down to them his mind was racing. It would seem that it was a mistake but Malcolm didn't really know Norberto. What if he was one sneaky little rascal who thought that he would be getting away with nicking the lot with just a few built holes in his leg. Besides, even if he were telling the truth they still had to find out who had their gear.

The doctor had done his job and said he needed to rest for now.

"He ain't resting just yet. Not till we find out a few things."

As the doctor left and said to drop the payment of as normal.

"It's not our fault and you understand why we have

done this to you don't you?"

Norbeto nodded, but as you can imagine, he didn't look too pleased. Once he and Malcolm had pinpointed where he had dropped the drugs on the map, they both realised it was the farm field just behind and not the one he was supposed to drop it in.

"You dropped it too early."

"Shit"

"Yes. Shit indeed."

"If this stuff isn't found you're in deep trouble my friend."

Johnny and Yang then went back to China Town to Wong's restaurant as Johnny had to lie low now ready to come see me.

So, with Johnny back in hiding, Malcolm sent some thugs to the farmhouse where they now believed the 20 keys must have been dropped. He had arranged for his mates daughter to see if the coast was clear.

Malcolm thought the farmer must still have it and knew they would have to act quickly if they were to get it back. Not many people would have had the money or the connections, to be able to shift that amount in the short time which had elapsed since the fuck up, unless they were connected to the streets somehow.

He was worried it could have fallen into the police's hands. Although, he reasoned, if it had been picked up by the old Bill, it probably would have been all over the news by now. Or it may mean the police could have set something up by putting something similar in the field to see who came to collect it. That would mean the police could be there waiting to arrest them.

Malcolm thought he was smarter than that, as he had

his mate's daughter ride her horse around the entire field to see if anyone was plotted up in the bushes, surrounding the field or to see if any police were camouflaged, sitting and waiting, but she saw no one and no sign of the old Bill or their agents.

Establishing that the coast was clear, Malcolm then picked up one of his minders and drove up to the farmhouse that the field belonged to with one of the heavies by his side ready to have a gentlemanly chat with the farmer. The farmer wasn't very responsive, as you could imagine. Malcolm wanted to try and get the stash back all nice and civilised but the farmer was having none of it.

Malcolm was careful and nice but firm about it all when he met and spoke to the farmer.

"Look, I know a hundred per cent that something that doesn't belong to you in any way shape or form has come into your field. This belongs to some good friends of mine but as you can now imagine, they aren't very happy that it's not here for me to pick up for them. They will stop at nothing, and I mean nothing, till they get it back. If you do the right thing and give it back to me, or tell me where I can get it back, then we will leave and no more will be said. I will be willing to give you £5,000 for your trouble as well".

He threw a crisp bundle of fifties onto the table in front of the farmer.

"If you take the money you will never see us again. Unless you want to rent your field out to us for other things. We can talk about that when we get the stuff back which I have come for. We would give you a few quid each time this happens in the future."

The farmer looked at the money on the table in front of him then looked at the menacing man standing at his table.

"Look, save us all a lot of tears," Malcolm's minder bellowed, "you would be wise to accept this offer. Otherwise certain things will happen. I would bet my money on that, these things will happen as there are a lot of lives at stake here. So, what I'm saying is this; if it doesn't come back you will not make it to the next harvest, do you know what I mean?"

"Look, I did find it but I have informed the police and they came round and have taken it away."

Malcolm looked at the minder and then back at the Farmer.

"Okay. Then what?"

"Sorry?"

"Well, what did they say?"

"They just took it away."

"Just like that? No questions asked? I ain't having that."

Malcolm picked up the money and placed it in his pocket.

"It seems as if you're wasting my time."

He knew there was no truth in the farmers words..

The farmer hadn't told the police at all. It was just a bluff to get Malcolm and the heavy men out of the farmhouse and off the scent. He had already sold it on for £30,000 large to Mr Khan. He knew he couldn't get it back even if he wanted to, but he could not tell them that or could he?

Before leaving Malcolm glanced around the room with highly attuned senses he observed the surroundings, noticing a nice old style shotgun. He shot a piercing gaze and shouted, "You're a silly old man. Very silly."

Walking out with the minder in tow he turns round to the farmer, "Nice shooter my friend!"

He then leaves shutting the door and talks to his minder; "I can tell he is shitting us."

"More like he's shitting himself."

Malcolm had to tell Mr Nice what had happened and how things had panned out. In turn Mr Nice had told the Liverpool Firm about their shipment going missing. It was then necessary for the Liverpool mob to put the Islington mob into the picture, after all they had put most of the money up for it for a cut of the cocaine.

Now they knew someone had had them over both Firms and Mr Nice wanted someone hurt for it or the money back within twenty-four hours. They weren't happy. Malcolm had said he had gone to talk to the farmer face-to-face but he had just mugged him off and he was having none of it.

"You went yourself? Are you fucking mad? Now we have no choice but to put a contract on the farmer as he has seen your face! Why didn't you send someone else for it? If he has gone to the police, he could and would be able to identify you now and put you up for it. Come on Malcolm! You need to fix up a little if you want to stay number one in the Firm mate. You need to be a bit sharper than that."

Mr Nice couldn't lose another front man.

He also knew he couldn't lose another person he trusted as he wouldn't be able to operate the way he was within the underworld having Johnny on the run.. Realising the severity of the situation, Mr Nice instructed the Liverpool mob that it was best to kill the Farmer. They put a hit on the farmer. The wheels had been put into motion just in case he had handed it in and was telling the truth. These guys weren't messing about.

A day after Malcolm's little visit, four masked men pulled up in a Land Rover sports. They got out and walked across some fields to the farmhouse, where they looked through the window and saw the farmer sitting there. The gunmen let off a few shots aimed at him through the window. After the third shot the gun was empty.

The other fellas ran around the farm looking for the parcel, but there was nothing.

"So, where is it?" the gunman demanded as he walked in and pointed the empty gun at the farmer from behind the banaclava. The farmer was up against the wall, bleeding from a bullet that had hit him.

"It's gone to my friend, the off licence owner Mr Khan a few shops down from the old bakery. Please help me, I feel cold."

"Terry?" one of the heavies called out to the trigger man as they all came in.

Terry turned to him.

"For fuck's sake! Are you fucking stupid? Come here!" He pushed him out of the way of everyone, "don't ever say my fucking name on a bit of work!"

"Calm down." The heavy turned back to the wounded farmer.

"You leave me no choice now," Terry then took the shotgun down and pointed it at the farmer. Blood started to poor out onto the floor as the farmer took his last breath and his eyes fixed.

"Well that's fucking great," said Terry.

The other masked man shouts out, "So how do we know where the parcel is now?"

"Look, we aren't here to find the drugs. We came to sort him out and that's what we have done. Anyway, he said it's with the off licence owner, name of Khan. He might be able to help us."

"Well, let's hope so."

"Look, we came here to kill him did we not? Now let's get the fuck out of here."

"How can we believe him?"

"Help me get him up."

"What? No, just leave him there and let's go."

"We ain't going anywhere till we sort this mess out."

They dragged the body out to the field close to the farm and placed the body on the stack the scarecrow was on and then placed the jacket on him and the hat and left the dead body propped up like he was the scarecrow as the other guy mopped up the blood splats from the bullet wound.

They then left, taking the shotgun with them, and walked across the fields back to the Land Rover. Before they drove away, the main masked man dug a shallow hole and placed the gun they had used in the shooting in the hole and pushed the dirt over it.

"Come on let's get the fuck out of here."

He placed the farmer's shotgun in the back of the Land Rover and covered it with a black sheet so if you did look in the boot, it just looked like the bare floor.

"You never know, we might need that one day."

They then removed their banaclavas and drove off.

CHAPTER 13

Mr Khan's sons were well connected to an Asian Firm in Bradford, who worked in the heroin and crack trade. They would be in a position to move that amount of drugs that their dad had given them from the botched up job in only a few months through their connections.

They were already well established in the street drug selling trade themselves and were washing cocaine into crack and were doing an okay trade. They had a team of shooters (street dealers) working and selling it for them.

As soon as Mr Khan had secured the 20 keys. He had given it to his eldest son Priesh, who was going out with a lovely Asian girl whose dad owned a cash and carry. Priesh was running for a Bradford Firm. They wanted to use their ill-gotten gains to buy his girlfriend's dad's cash and carry in order to put there drug money through. They wanted it bad! But it wasn't for sale.

So now, the drugs were with Priesh, who had then passed them on to the Bradford Firm he was mixed up with. These drugs acted as part payment to his own drug debts as he too was a crack smoker. Mr Khan figured he was helping

Priesh get out of the debt, he hated the thought of his son owing these guys anything. He longed for his whole family to be back on the straight and narrow. He didn't know the extent of the trouble Priesh was in with his crack habit but he hoped that by giving Priesh the drugs to sell on would ease his troubles with the Bradford Firm.

He had given them the drugs on cheap with a reasonable profit, which had made evened things out between them, till the police raided his flat and caught his younger brother with 3 guns they had stashed there for the Bradford Firm. He was supposed to be hiding the guns for them, so now, he owed them for that, so the drugs were sold for a speedy and tidy return but there was still an unwanted debt to pay.

They paid back to their father by some of the money that had been made. Mr khan had intended to use this little bit of money to square up with the farmer, but of course he couldn't pay the farmer back now because after all, he was still scaring crows. That's not strictly speaking true. The farmer's body had been found by the police and the farm was taped off and was now crawling with forensic teams. The UK media were all over this story like a rash.

Mr Khan now knew he had to move fast and would have to leave the area. So he took the money owed and invested in a timeshare property in Spain. He had buried the rest of it in the garden for safe keeping. He now thought the owner of the drugs had come to see the farmer and he didn't know how safe he would be and didn't want to be the next story in the news.

The Bradford mob still wanted the money for the guns taken by the police from Priesh's younger brothers flat which they had asked him to look after. So, the Bradford mob knowing he didn't have any money, told him he must start putting pressure on his girlfriend to persuade her old man to sell them his cash and carry. At first Priesh refused, but they kept on at him, calling and harassing him all the time at the Mosque. They laid it on Priesh thick- they kept saying shit like; its bro's before hoe's, women come and go, brothers are for eternity -you're in with us or you're out.

His loyalty was with the Firm and not with his girlfriend whose name was Mia as she had now had a inclining that Priesh was a drug addict but at this time she was standing by him until he started to turn. As I said, the Bradford mob were desperate to gain control of the cash and carry on many occasions and they would come and offer him silly money but he didn't want dirty drug money and it was a family business past down from generation to generation.

"Look, I'm not selling this place. You're wasting your time."

Undeterred, the Bradford mob came back every week and tried to intimidate him and would offer him more and more money. Having chosen his allegiance to lay with the Bradford mob, Priesh was now being incredibly horrible to Mia.

He was under a shit load of pressure as he had now also fallen behind with payments and other things. Priesh understood that if he didn't do as he was told, he would wind up working with so many others addicts who were in the Bradford mobs debt. Many of whom were now compelled to rob prostitutes in sex flats. Just so they could stay ahead.

The Bradford mob also had another element to keep Priesh doing what they wanted. His younger brother was banged up and they had people on the inside putting the poor fucker through hell. He didn't want his brother to suffer any more in prison, and the mob had contacts inside that would do as they were told, so he was trapped between trying to get the cash and carry from his girlfriend's dad and keeping his brother stuck in prison safe. Like they kept saying *'women come and go. Friends don't and brothers stick together'.*

Mia came to the entrance of their flat as she had returned home earlier than expected. She noticed the main fella of the Bradford Firm leaving. Walking into the flat she caught Priesh bending down snorting a line of cocaine from their table.

Priesh looked up. He was surprised. Mia never left work this early and wondered why she was home. Seeing Priesh doing this had proved he hadn't given it up and was still taking drugs confirming her suspicions. In her head now this was the last straw as of late, Priesh had been giving her so much pressure and telling so many lies and was trying to manipulate her. And here he was doing drugs in their flat.

She asked him to stop doing the drugs and also asked him to stop harassing her dad. Cocked up and furious, Priesh began pushing her out the way so he could get to the drugs that were in a bag on the table.

Mia screamed at him picking up the bag of drugs.

"You don't understand, I need this Mia so that I can get my money back and get people off my back and buy you the things you want."

"What by taking it? Can't you see it's messing you up?"

"The drugs are okay when you're spending and spending the fucking money, but when we I have to pay for them back and all I ask is that you ask your dad to sell up, you're nowhere to be seen and you think I'm being unreasonable."

She opened her purse.

"Here, take your money back." She took off her top. "And have this back as well if it came from your drug money!" As she slung the Gucci top to his face, she tipped the bag of powder onto the floor.

"That's what I think of drugs. Don't you get it? Drugs are for mugs, and you're the mug involved in it all. You're too stupid to say no and you let them suck you in more and more. Look at you, you're a mess."

He back handed her and gave her a big black eye.

"You do as you're told; otherwise they will kill me and my brother. You don't know what they are like. After all I have done for you!"

Mia fell on to the sofa and cried.

CHAPTER 14

Back to yours truly!

I thought a night out would do me good.

Old School and I met up at the Ministry of Sound night club. Old School had introduced me to Jenny who was the venue's host and also to the other DJs and various promoters. Jenny had introduced me to her mate, this Mia. She turned out to be this pretty Asian woman that was getting a hard time from her boyfriend. Mia began to tell me the story that he was now mixed up with a big Asian Firm in Bradford. After spending half the night chatting with them both while Old School was doing his set on the decks. I felt like I had known both girls for ages. When Jenny went to the toilet leaving me alone with Mia, I asked her to tell me the details.

That's how I knew what was going on in her life and what had happened with Priesh and the Bradford mob.

I couldn't help noticing whilst talking with her how her beauty was tarnished with a beast of a shiner on her right eye, "What happened to your eye, if you don't mind me asking?"

She blushed.

"I was just wondering why a good looking girl like you has a black eye. Not into boxing are you?"

She sort of smiled.

"No, far from it."

I took a sip of the champagne from the ice bucket that had wine, vodka and juice complimentary from the club for Old School and Jenny.

I could see she had tried to hide her black eye as best she could with her hair and make-up.

She took a deep breath and came out with it. It looked painful. Whoever had hit her, had hit her fucking hard.

"It's a long story and would take ages to tell and I don't want to involve anyone in my problems."

This made me curious and I wanted to know more.

"Well, I have all night and now we're here talking about it." I leant back in the chair and continued. "I guess I'm already involved."

She smiled and moved nearer to me so I could hear her better over the music while she spoke. I would look up at her every now and then and look around at my surroundings as the lights flashed around us, watching the dancers, then I would concentrate on what she was telling me. I poured more champagne into both of our glasses.

As the alcohol flowed Mia started to feel more comfortable in my company and began to open up more about what had happened to her. Jenny had re-joined us again and picked up the glass of champagne saying, "Cheers."

Then Jenny joined our conversation. Mia expressed her regret about getting involved with Priesh as he has changed since he got himself involved with this gang in

Bradford. His life had spiralled out of control since he had gotten mixed up in drugs and all the other criminal things they were into.

Mia told me her story and it felt as though we had known each other for ever. It was clear to me that Mia was desperate for the situation to be sorted. She motioned that her dad was being hassled by this gang.

"My family thought he was a nice lad and they helped us get together. But all the time the gang are trying to bully him and in turn he bullies me to get my dad to sell the family business to them. Once, things went wrong for them and his brother got arrested."

"Why don't he just sell it then they'll go away?"

"It's the only thing keeping dad alive and it was passed onto him by his mum and has been like this for years, passed down from my family."

Heritage - man, cross cultures, and forever and always, that's some heavy obligation we all bow down to, Mia went on, "We seemed okay for a bit then they all turned on us. He has messed up with them, something to do with losing some heroin and guns that the police found at one of his brother's properties. The police had seized possession of the flat and arrested his younger brother and they lost the lot because they all had put money into the property and the drugs as well. So when things had gone wrong for them, they had then found out he was going out with me and that my dad owned a cash and carry shop and now they want it in return for the mess up. Their mum can't be here unless she has some business ties here so getting this would help them. They say it was my ex-boyfriend's brother's fault they lost the flat and that if they bought the cash and carry off my dad, then all would be okay again between them all, minus the outstanding that they lost out on. My dad and all of our family have worked hard for this shop. If we lose it for some drug debt, then we're finished. I didn't want to help my ex out and definitely not the gang out by doing that to my dad. Selling the family shop to them they said that my ex owes them and that I am with him so I should help him pay it off by helping them get the cash and carry. Just as a loyal wife-to-be should help her man, but not at the cost of my own family."

Mia paused and I could tell she was trying hard to fighting the tears, "It's such a mess and if I go to the police, then things will just get worse. So, we just kept arguing over it and all of a sudden it came, whap, he hit me. And that was it; he said I would do as I was told. After that I would not answer his calls. He came and saw me and apologised to me but I had had it with him, with the drugs, the Firm, the lot. He was letting the gang force my dad in to selling the cash and carry. I left the next day taking all my stuff and went back to Jenny's but they keep coming and pestering dad in turn."

"That's bad mate. Really bad."

"Yes it is."

I picked up my glass and then took a sip, looking around the club at everyone's dancing to the banging beats.

My attention was bought back to Mia once she said that they had got a lot of cocaine from their dad that owned an off licence with the money he had got back he had got this timeshare in Spain and then buried a few quid in the garden. Then my ears pricked up. I wanted to know more about the cocaine. She continued now having my full attention once the cocaine word had been uttered.

"Priesh's dad had loads of cocaine somehow. He had

given it to his son to pay back the debt to the Bradford mob hoping they would go away. I was going mad at him bringing his drugs and using it in our house. She paused, sighing, "Look, I wish I hadn't told you now."

"Look, it's cool mate.

So, after that night's clubbing, we exchanged numbers. I told Old School about it all as I knew he fancied the pants off Jenny, the club promoter, but hadn't had it off with her yet. If he could help Mia out, we knew it would give him some brownie points with Jenny. So, I told him and Jenny confirmed all that Mia had told us. Old School said to leave it with him.

"I'll talk to someone about it." He was good like that. Old School was one of those people who knew someone who knew someone, you know?

He told Wong about the cocaine load the off licence owner seemed to have stumbled on and the other bits about Mia, but Wong wasn't interested at all but just the cocaine. He said he couldn't help as there was nothing in it for him. Yang was there and heard everything and she knew the cocaine was the stuff they had tried to get back from the farmer and the pilot.

She then told Johnny the hit man, as he was still alive at the time, and was only at the restaurant, lying low, waiting for Mandy's funeral to take place..

Then Johnny had told his mate, the Sicilian mob boss, about the money at the timeshare and he knew it would come in handy if he could get his hands on it. They had become good friends after Johnny had done a hit on some fella that was in prison by shooting him from a distance with a high powered rifle, hitting the fella in the prison yard. The Firm wanted him dead and they had been paying money out to other inmates to kill him, but they were just hurting him, till Johnny was recommended and got involved. Johnny didn't fuck about. You'd think you would be safe in prison wouldn't you? But for some of us, it's worse than being free and on the outside.

So, within time, the Sicilian mob boss had found out about the Asian Firm in Bradford and what they were doing to Mia. He didn't care about that, but it was the money he was interested in. I had asked Mia how much they wanted to pay for the cash and carry. She had told me.

"So, where did they get the money from?" I guessed it was drugs that they got off her ex's dad the off license owner. She confirmed all the details and the dots were completing the picture now, lucky Mr Khan and his not so lucky family!

Old School told Wong, who told us to stay out of it and the minder then told Johnny to sort out a deal which was set to meet up with the Bradford fellas, of course all of this went through Mr Nice who oversaw everything!

The Mafia mob boss had told Yang to arrange for the same men who had seen to the farmer to pay Mr Khan a visit and to make sure that what was being said was true, as he was also friends with the Liverpool mob.

They pulled up, got out of the van and walked in. They dragged Mr Khan out of the back of his off licence while one of them stood at the door and had turned the sign on it to shut, while they were all wearing banaclavas ready to confront him. They sat him on a chair and threatened to pour petrol all over him as they splashed some around the back and on the stove they then light a fag and popped it in his mouth knowing that if he dropped it, he would go up in flames! Ominously, one of his assailants growled,

"Are you ready to tell us or shall we walk away?" Fag in

mouth, Mr Khan could only mumble. In one swift motion one of the banaclava goons removed the cigarette.

Petrified Mr Khan spewed his guts out. He told them all about passing the drugs to his sons to help them and that he knew that it wouldn't be too long before someone came after him now that the farmer was dead. He knew too much already. He said that he had given the drugs to his sons who were well connected to the Bradford Firm. He had sworn on his life that he wouldn't tell his sons that someone had paid him a visit. Almost weeping, Mr Khan explained that he had some of the money for the drugs as it was buried in the timeshare, they could have it all if they just left him alone.

To make sure he knew they meant business; the thugs poured petrol over the entire off licence and then set fire to the shop. It burned down but they had let him slip out the back. They then had his car smashed to bits and said,

"Things can get a lot worse, so you keep your fucking mouth shut." They then dropped him off at a bus stop.

His sons thought it was a racial attack and that's what Mr Khan had said when he questioned by the police. He knew it was the right thing to say if he wanted to stay alive. In a way, they had let him off lightly. The thugs with Yang had passed on all the information to Johnny who had started to plan things with the Mafia mob boss.

Mr Khan went back to India for his own safety until the boys could get the cash and carry sorted, then he could sort the mess out they were all in. He also told Johnny and the Sicilian mob about the money buried in the timeshare and that his son had the key. The Bradford Firm was now trying to get a load more drugs to make more money, as now one of their drug sellers had been caught driving on the M25 with five keys of heroin and was on remand for it.

They were now desperate to make money with whoever had drugs for sale and who were willing to lie some on too as they thought they might be able to knock them for it. They had spoken to Mia when they conveniently bumped into her outside work. They had pulled up in their Mercedes as she walked along the street and they started hassling her again.

"Mia, look life could be easy for you and your family. Why make it hard for yourself? Just do the right thing and your dad will have money and he can then move on and that boyfriend of yours can walk the streets feeling safe again." The Bradford mob pulled up.

"Look go away and leave me alone. We will never sell it to you."

"Mia, come on now, once we've managed to get another load of drugs sorted you know we will be buying the place off your dad whether you like it or not. So unless you don't want to see him hurt, you'd best tell him to accept this last offer as my patience has run out."

They then went to town smashing up her flat and beating Priesh up. He called Mia to help him but all she could do was sob in the corner. They had went to the cash and carry to see her dad. He had tried to stop them from taking things but he was impotent against such wanton violence! The members of the Bradford mob smashed the cameras with their bats and had caused a mess and they took all the money out of the tills.

He was overwhelmed and had been punched and kicked in the scuffle they had had in the shop.

"Stay there old man. This is my place and I'll do and take what I like."

"You'll be paid soon," the main Asian Firm member said, "So we are not stealing from you. Think of it as a little protection money and if we own this place, then we're only just taking what's ours."

He walked out of the cash and carry shop, leaving the poor old man defeated, prostrate on the floor, soaking wet.

Once the Bradford Firm could get their hands on some more drugs they then could buy this cash and carry. Mia had told me what had happened to her dad. I then repeated it all to Old School and once again, in turn, Old School had told it to Wong.

"Just leave it, it's not our business, forget about it," were Wong's words.

Wong then passed the story on to Johnny who was still hiding at Wong's place waiting for Mandy's funeral and he had run it all past his mate the Sicilian Mafia boss for advice on what the best thing to do. They decided they wanted the money that was buried in the time share. Johnny was talking with them through his cousin's barbers in Oxford Street while still laying low in Soho.

The Mafia mob man had come over and was sitting in the chair next to Johnny while they got their hair cut and they talked business with regards to what was to happen next with this Bradford mob-money, money, money. These guys wanted that stashed of dough like you couldn't believe!

Johnny didn't want to get involved at first until Wong had asked and they had first gone to see the pilot. So, the Sicilian Mafia mob boss had talked to Johnny and said it could be a paying job with a little bit of juggling around.

"We could kill two birds with one stone; help your friend Old School out, let him think we sorted the problem, but he won't know about the money. Then we can get the money from the timeshare."

So, he then sorted out a meeting by telling Wong to

get Old School to instruct Mia to set up a meeting with the Bradford Firm. I passed the information on. Mia was told to arrange a meeting with them and she promised she would to talk to the Bradford Firm.

"Look, I can help you out with some drugs if you leave me alone. I can help you where the drugs were concerned." She told her ex when he told her they had been putting pressure on him to steal drugs from dealers and from the prostitutes flats and deals they had set up and had been paid for. He had been picked up outside the Mosque and was told to rob a few dealers, but that wasn't enough for them. They needed another load of drugs again to get them started and to be able to give Mia's dad the money for the cash and carry.

Mia told all this to me and Old School while we were at her Auntie's Indian restaurant having a bite to eat. Jenny was from the Ministry night club was also there. She had heard that Old School liked her and wanted to help, so she wanted to try and get Old School residency at the club as the owner Jack had said, Old School was doing well and everyone wanted DJ Mad, AKA Old School, at the Club. He had been pulling in the raving crowds and he wanted to get residency in Jenny's pants too and at her house if things went as planned. With many hidden agendas bubbling under the surface we offered Mia the following bits of advice.

"Look, tell them we can help them with the drugs they're looking for," we told her, just as the message had been laid back to us from Wong, from the Mafia. So Mia had spoken to her ex.

"I will help you get out of this mess. Just do as I ask."

He then spoke to the Bradford mob who then asked to see her. She went to speak to them.

"Please, if you stop the Firm from hurting my dad then I know where you can get some more drugs." This was what Johnny and the Sicilian Mafia mob boss wanted her to say, as they had discussed in his cousin's barbers in Oxford Street. That's what she was told to tell them, that she knew someone who had access to a lot of drugs by the people who brought it over themselves. They had asked how she knew this and she said she had met these people at the club.

"You know where Jenny works, at the Ministry, you know the one Jack runs?" She told them that the fellas she had met one night had got talking a little too much to try to impress her about a big drugs deal they were going to do soon.

"Who are they?" they asked.

"Well one is a DJ there." She showed him the flyer where DJ Mad Al, AKA Old School, was on the top line up. "The other one is his mate, the Cookster. They were talking to me and Jenny about how they knew these Sicilian fellas that had access to a load of drugs. They were saying it to try and impress us. You know Jenny the club's promoter? My friend, the blonde one that looks after the guest list at the door. I think this DJ Old School really fancies Jenny badly. Well they said that they are going to do a big cocaine deal."

She told them the time and place Wong had told us. The bait was set and these big old fish were nibbling. They were getting sucked in well and truly. Mia had executed her role perfectly and now the trap had been laid.

When Mia told us she had set the trap, we informed Wong.

"Okay fellas, your bits done. Leave the rest to me and they will get it sorted."

"Really?" Old school asked.

"Trust me!"

Old School and I just sat back and waited. Wong had passed the details to Johnny who had sorted a meeting with the Sicilian mob boss and his friend.

We weren't there but knew from Wong they would be sorted and they would soon leave Mia and her dad alone.

CHAPTER 15

Within time, Johnny backed into the scrap yard in an old Merc and the Sicilian man pulled in behind him in an Escort van. Now, the drug deal they were doing was real but they wanted to kill two birds with one stone. Johnny opened the boot as the Sicilian mob boss opened the two doors to the Escort van and began loading boxes into the Merc. They then passed over a sports bag of money and shut the doors. They shook hands that's when it happened.

The Asian Firm sprang from behind the cars wearing hoodies and caps holding baseball bats. There were three of them. Another pulled up in an old Datsun car. The biggest Asian body-builder came forward and spoke from behind his scarf.

"Don't try anything funny otherwise we'll kill you both."

Johnny looked at him and raised his eyebrows. The Asian man came forward and swung the bat at Johnny. Johnny dodged it and grabbed the bat out of his hand. With all the power he had, Johnny wacked the bat across the top of his head, knocking him out. He then threw the bat to one side.

"Who's next?"

He pulled off his coat and threw it on the seat of the Merc.

"Fuck this," the mafia boss said. "I ain't got time for this bollocks."

He pulled out his gun and shot them. Bang … Bang … Bang.

"Fuck the lot of you." He shouted letting off shot after shot. They fell to the floor. He walked over to them and said, "Okay," addressing the main fella who was trying to start the car. "So, where's this money?"

"What money?" He shot him again, this time in the hand. He then told him to get out the car and lay down on the floor. He stood on his arm.

"The money you got for the stolen cocaine."

In mortal agony, whimpering like a shitting dog, he screamed, "It's in the timeshare in Marbella. Here's the address. Here's the fucking key, just let me go and I'll keep quiet about all this." Smirking to himself the Sicilian boss, known by his mother as Franco and to every other sucker as Don F, turned languidly to face Johnny, before swivelling to deliver another fateful shot.

Don F then helped Johnny put them into the boot of the smashed Datsun and told their friend in the digger crane to lift the car. He then let it go in the squashing machine, pulled it out and released it into the freshly dug hole. Then the dirt was pushed over it.

Johnny had quickly deposited the gun in a dumpster and got in to the Mercedes with Don F. They drove out of the scrap yard, leaving the Escort there with no number plates, ready to be scrapped. They then drove to Kilburn and dropped the real drugs off into the basement of some restaurant.

The other son that was connected to the Bradford mob didn't know that they had just done their last deal with Don F. He himself was sitting outside an Asian restaurant, smoking on a hookah, as they drove past and let him have it.

Once the Sicilian mob had the money dug up from the timeshare as agreed with Johnny, they would keep half and give the rest back to Mr Nice for a stake in his Colombian field. Johnny had told him all about Mr Nice and what he was doing out there at the time. He said he had one more thing to do in England then he would be out of here and back in Barbados, or he could meet him in Spain and dig the money up from the timeshare and share it out.

Don F said he could do it for him for old time's sake. Now they were partners in this money, he said he would help him. He and Johnny, didn't know just yet that the cocaine field had been sprayed and was no good, not to man nor beast.

Ignorant of the actual scenario and all the many nefarious moves that Mr Nice was involved with, Johnny and Don F agreed to part ways and meet up later at the address given for the timeshare property.

Meanwhile, the Liverpool mob wanted to get their revenge for the debacle of the plan drop. As you know, they had put their money where their mouths were for this one. So, Mr Nice said,

"It's no good shouting at me. Sort it out your fucking selves," knowing very well that they would get rid of poor Norberto once and for all, meaning he wouldn't have to worry about the Colombians trying to contact him.

"I have enough on my plate trying to get the next drops sorted for you fellas."

"Well, I'm just saying he was done by us for the fuck up."

"It was the pilot's fuck up not mine, so do what you must."

"Well, he's still walking around, or should I say wobbling around, like Jack the lad."

"Do something about it then if you're not happy," Mr Nice said, "stop wasting my time. You'll be contacted once the next lot is in place okay?"

The Liverpool mob then took Norberto out of the game. They had beaten him to a pulp and thrown him in a container in the German man's shipping yard because one of them was going out with the German's daughter, unbeknown to Mr Nice. Mr Nice was now trying to get him to come and meet Curtis with the rest of the cocaine still stashed in Colombia.

Norberto became part of the cargo and was shipped out to China where he was arrested by the immigration officers who had found him fighting for his life. Fritz, the shipping yard manager was a good friend of Mr Nice's now and Wong's minder had persuaded him to help out. Not many people knew this till now as he had a thing for her and she liked him too.

So, she had fucked him for the Firm and also for herself and then in the moment of passion, she pulled her own shooter, turned it on him and told him what he would do. Now that's loyalty, and as you can now see men are weak when it comes to pussy and confronted with the barrel of a gun. She told him he will do it otherwise he will feel what it is like to be a woman. She pointed the gun at his cock in a seductive way. Fritz immediately rang Wong and had said he would try to sort things out but things like this took time and a lot of planning and he said he needed money as man can't live on air alone. If they wanted the cocaine, he was the man to do it.

The Chinese police held Norberto in custody as he didn't have any papers or anything on him. He was arrested black and blue, with a bullet hole in his leg and no papers to prove how or why he was there. They opened the container and found him nearly half dead and couldn't work out why he was in the container in the first place.

He wasn't answering any of their questions once in the interview room, which was making his position much worse, so the police decided to keep him in custody for his own safety and had had an investigation put out to find out why he was in there and to find out what shipping yard the container came from.

When they had found this out they had also found out that he was connected to the Colombians. That was the last call that had come through on his phone. The police had then gone to Elstree Aerodrome and seized the plane. Until the police could find out who he really was or where he was really from and why he had flown over here there speculations and conjecture amounted to so much bull shit!

They thought he must have been flying money, drugs or immigrants over. He was threatening to go to the police to Mr Nice after he wrongly got shot in his legs unless Mr Nice gave him a big back hander for letting him get shot in the first place and he was also going to tell the Colombians that he would hand them over if they didn't pay him.

Mr Nice thought, *Fuck this, no one blackmails me, and certainly not some pussy pilot.* He didn't want to be held at ransom by anyone, so one smart move and he had killed two birds with one stone by telling the Liverpool mob to sort him out themselves.

The deal was set by Mia and the Sicilian mob and Johnny had taken care of them and they were just waiting to go over to the timeshare unbeknownst to me and Old School as we had no idea Johnny was even in England. They were going to dig up the money, but first he wanted to go to his sister's funeral and bury me too for not looking after her.

The next thing I knew I was at Mandy's funeral. We were all standing there with villains and gangsters of all sorts of calibre from all over Essex, London, Manchester, Liverpool and a few faces from Ireland and Scotland. As I looked down into Mandy's grave and at her coffin I was gutted. I had fancied the pants off her from the moment I saw her. I thought, as it all became a blur, if we had just had some more time I know I would have cracked it instead of getting her killed.

I looked up and out the corner of my eye I saw Wong's Bentley slowly drive up the road to where we were standing on the edge by the graves. I thought it was nice of Wong to turn up. Yang and George, the fella that had driven the dusk cart that we had escaped Mr B from, had gotten out of the front and walked to the back to open the door and out got a tall, well-dressed man in a black trench coat wearing Armani sunglasses looking for all the world like Al Pacino. That's when it clicked.

Fuck me, it was Johnny!

My heart sank and my breathing sped up. I knew this was it for me. Johnny was here and I was a dead man. I was scared. It wasn't worth running. I was here in the shadows of the dead and now I was about to join them.

He walked over to the grave as they were lowering Mandy into the freshly dug hole everything started to go in slow motion. He threw a white rose and a photo of the family on top of the coffin.

The photo captured Johnny, his old man, the casino

owner, and his mum and Mandy. As it came to rest on top of the coffin he looked up and then slowly looked at me and put his hands into the side of his trench coat, ready to pull out a shooter. He took off his glasses and placed them in his pocket and then just stared at me.

Old School knew what was about to happen next and there was nothing he could do to stop Johnny from killing me. Johnny went to withdraw his hand. All of a sudden the whole place erupted with police.

"Johnny Massiny, stay where you are don't move. It's the police."

Johnny left whatever was in his pocket in there, jumped over the grave, and ran past me as the police followed in pursuit. Then, as we got close again, Johnny was on the floor bleeding from his wound the police gunshot made. He lay there with the police all around him. He just gave me a cold stare and then died before my very eyes. One of the police officers searched Johnny and pulled a semi-automatic Makarov pistol from his pocket.

That's when I knew Johnny would have killed me for sure if he had had the chance. We hadn't heard from Mr Nice for some time so we had to tell Mr Nice what had happened.

"Hi, Old School don't tell me Johnny's killed the Cookster for getting Mandy killed."

"Well that will be hard mate, as Johnny is dead too." That's when Mr Nice went quiet.

"Dead …" It was neither a question nor a statement just a solemn appreciation for the reality of the scenario.

Old School went on,

"Yes the police were waiting for him at Mandy's funeral, they shot him and have took photos of all that attended. A few others are now slipping off to court or out of the country to Puerto Buenos and Cyprus."

Mr Nice put the phone down and knew things would change now Johnny was gone and that the police would be crawling all over the Firm. If they had been at the funeral then they were on his tail. He needed to move the rest of the stolen cocaine and fast.

CHAPTER 16

Looking back I realise that that's why I too had been invited to the nightclub for the meeting with Mr Nice after leaving the police station to also meet more villains and gangsters. This was a new world order. We were advised we should also bring our women. They wanted to make it look as informal as possible and it would look like more of a social gathering and not a villains and gangsters get together if we were being monitored, which by now was well on the cards after what had gone down.

So, doing it like this at the club, we didn't look like a load of villains and gangsters, instead it would seem to be just good old boys out on a jolly so we couldn't get nicked for the association.

That night Mr Nice one again, as always, was laid on by his contacts, only he would not be attending. He had sent someone to be there for him, his close old friend Malcolm. That's how we got to meet him. Well they met him - I just shook his hand.

Malcolm had done a small bit of business with Mr Nice many years ago in old East End. His daughter had been going out with an American guy from Miami. This meant he was also well connected even before Mr Nice introduced Malcolm to his own little Firm back then. He still had a contact for them, but hadn't been in touch and would only contact them again when desperate.

They were also a staunch Firm in their own right. They had stayed in touch, but now Johnny was gone he had offered Malcolm the job as the main man in this Firm. He trusted him and his empire had grown a lot since they had met in person. However, they had stayed in contact on the phone and had met up at his friend's casino from time to time to play and talk business. He was also an accountant, which came in very handy.

This last formal meeting was arranged by Mr Nice as one before the next things that happened. He had invited only his closest associates. He wanted those that he had picked close and the rest out of the way before 'they' brought the whole organisation down.

Malcolm now being in the position as Mr Nice's new number one, was taking care of the Firm's business and would soon be going to see Mr B but this was going to be kept quiet from all of us here. This was Mr Nice's new focus as you can recall he wanted his dollar and couldn't get it without that number.

As if everyone knew about this plan, we too would want a cut as we would jump on the bandwagon and say we would help and get involved, even if we didn't need to be. Malcolm was instructed to chat to those that were still involved and those that were still connected in some way or another to Mr Nice's Firm and to introduce himself to them so they knew who was boss. It was best for all of us to meet at this club. They sort of half-owned it and were getting a cut from the bar's takings. So it made sense to meet there.

Malcolm wanted to give everyone the heads up on how things would work now and that any business arrangements went through him now and in turn they would get dealt with by Mr Nice and Wong. That's the way Mr Nice wanted it all to work and if anyone didn't like it then they should fuck off. It was getting too risky with everything that had gone down so far and those that were still getting pulled in.

They would no longer be welcome, no matter what they thought they brought to the table. Old School had asked me to come along to the meeting that night, which was why Vivian and I found ourselves sitting there at the Firm's table. As he said, it would be good to meet some more faces. So, we had sat at the table with a few other glamorous, high maintenance girls. . They were obviously the gangsters' molls and they sat next to us. Also, sat at our table were some more of Britain's most wanted. Some real dangerous men that I had only read about in books and seen on Crime watch until now.

CHAPTER 17

Things were coming on top for us all now that we had all been spotted at the funeral. The link between us and the police had been made and we were now all being investigated. They knew it was only a matter of time, and for some reason they seemed to know a lot more than we thought. Johnny had been killed and a few of us had been pulled in and questioned. This meant the police files were growing by the day. With all these things going on and the new evidence coming to light, new arrests were taking place and giving light to new evidence, which meant many leads for the police to follow up on and finally catching up with other members that we may have worked with in the past.

The police wanted Mr Nice badly. It was all since the driver had gotten away with the cocaine. It didn't make sense as no one else had seen him. He had disappeared, but from that day it seemed the police were well on us. It seemed they wanted us all desperately, Mr Nice most of all, but they just couldn't get anything on him or to get anything to stick that would put him away long enough.

They seemed to know he was the one, the main fella,

but he was covering his steps well and they needed proof, hard facts actually. They were now finding out just how well-connected Johnny had become, and that Mr Nice was somewhere behind it all.

Yeah, the Police knew of Mr Nice but at this time they just couldn't join the dots. Mr Nice was smart enough to keep it that way. So, when the police did come looking in his direction, once again they would find nothing to follow their suspicions on, and the trail to Mr Nice would go cold. So, to cut ties with certain people and to be out of the way but still call the shots was pretty smart. He hadn't risen to the top for nothing!

Maybe the diver I had met had it, but he was still long gone and no one seemed to have seen or heard from him. Maybe, they had gotten to him and he had done the talking to expose the Firm and was now in a safe house under police protection. Once the police had the evidence and could prove it, armed with this evidence they would see everyone go down for a long time.

They had their ideas but needed some good strong evidence that would stand up in court and convict not only Mr Nice, but all the main players in the Firm. They needed a strong witness to back the evidence up as well, and to get that in the realms we worked in was like finding a four-leaf clover.

Some of their evidence was just superficial and hearsay, but if they could get a Firm witness to testify against Mr Nice, then it would be taken as factual. They could then link us all together and prove everything against us so that even the best barrister in the land would not be able to save us with points of law no matter how much they were offered. No amount of legal bullshit and pontificating can surmount a good eye witness grass job!

Then for sure we would all be behind bars.

CHAPTER 18

I was at the club now on this meeting, like I say, the whole dynamics of the Firm had changed and no one could stop it, no matter how high up the ladder they were, or thought they were. Now Johnny was gone it was a whole different ball game in the underworld and the police knew it. There was nothing anyone in the Firm could do unless they knew how to resurrect Johnny, or replace him with a man of the same calibre. Which meant having men that will kill for the right price, and they are hard to find. You could get a drug addict to do the dirty work for a small fee, or for their next fix, which sometimes happens.

Other members of the Firm had also been banged up now, whether they had a direct involvement with the Firm or a link to it in some way other than drugs, and they too were being asked if they knew a man called The Milkman, which is what they had nicknamed Mr Nice. They had evidence that he had been called this in the past.

I'm telling you these were hectic days, even some of the top players were now coming unstuck and were drawn in to do their bit of bird after years and years of getting away with loads, and I mean loads, of skulduggery. The super forces had now caught up with them too.

They had performed years and years of close-knit investigations. A lot of hard work and many, many man-hours of surveillance team work had gone down in order to infiltrate and catch the main players within the drugs trade and organised crime which I now found myself involved in once again. The police were pulling us in and arresting us on silly charges just to have us behind bars, or else in the hope of getting a name or a place dropped unknowingly by the interviewee.

Arrests were also being made in international waters and all over London. The police had also set up entrapments all around London and other well-known areas in the UK where drugs, criminality and anti-social behaviour were renowned!

By doing this the pigs had meant a big crack down on drug trafficking and crime in general throughout the whole world, not just in the UK, leaving Mr Nice's Firm shocked at the way things had gone.

Criminal rackets, drug smuggling, prostitution rings, money laundering, you name it, they were all being brought down faster by the police, with more raids being done on different properties and businesses all over England and overseas.

With the breakthroughs in new technology, it meant that people that worked with and for Mr Nice in one way or another would all have to be very careful and have to keep well on their toes. We would have to be a lot smarter now with the things we were all getting up to, and this meant cutting ties with each other, if we were to stand a chance of not getting caught.

We had to play at the top of our game. Fix up and look sharp. This meant not driving about in flash cars, getting jobs and dressing in line with everyone else, and in some cases still renting the houses we had and thinking about where we could keep the money safe.

The police were also on top of the money-laundering - well some of it - so we had to go underground and be far more careful then we had ever been before if we didn't want to get nicked and go down for a long time.

As you know, Johnny had been Mr Nice's henchman hit man. He had been the enforcer, the man who collects the debts owed by other Firms. He was every other Firm's nemesis. Now he was out of the way, Mr Nice would have to lean more on his brother Hector who owned a security Firm. Hector lived in Cyprus, from time to time in order to try and hold the Firm together before it crumbled and everyone else started fighting for sole position.

CHAPTER 19

As you know, me and Viv had arrived at the club that infamous night. We said we were there to see Old School, which was true. He had told me to say that when we arrived at the doors of the club. The club was in Leicester Square. The two doormen then led me and Viv to the other face's table.

"This is Andy B. He is one of yours." The doorman then walked back over to the foyer.

"Hi, I'm Andy B. Any friend of Old Schools is a friend of mine. He'll be here soon. Come this way mate."

"This is Vivian, Andy."

"Nice to meet you darling," he shouted over the music. "Here, have a seat and make yourselves comfortable. This is my table. Anything you want, just help yourselves." The table in front of us was fully stocked with drinks; wines, vodka, fruit juice and a massive bottle of champagne on a silver base with strawberry's and jugs of soft drinks. Andy filled both our glasses with champagne. Remembering my manners I said,

"Thanks Andy."

It felt nice sitting there above the dance floor, looking

down and having the VIPs dancing around us.

"Not a problem mate, Old School speaks very highly of you."

"He's a great fella Andy."

"Enough said. You're amongst friends here son, so just keep your head down and enjoy yourself. I know all about what you have done for the Firm, so all is good mate."

"I have seen you before. You were at the strip bar when we all met up and then went back to the hotel for some cabaret. You were with Old School then before you had met your lovely lady."

He laughed,

"I remember now, I was well wrecked."

"We all were mate. You left early as you got a little paranoid."

We were shouting over the music as one of the girls at the table asked Viv,

"Got a light sweetheart?"

"Sorry, don't smoke."

"I've been trying to give it up," sighed the girl, "Want to go to the bathroom? Fancy a line?" She stood up.

"No thanks," Viv replied.

Andy shouted over into my ear,

"We're just waiting on Old School to arrive, and this Malcolm fella too." Who was Malcolm? I hadn't heard of him before tonight. We were sitting at a table with a few other villains and faces that I didn't know, but was now getting introduced to by Andy for some reason.

"This is Dave D; they call him The Slipper King." It was the nickname he had been given when he was working at a strip club in Park Royal after they had stopped working at the Gas club. He was always in a suit and wore slippers like he owned the place. A nice fella, but not to those who got on his wrong side. Like all villains and gangsters, he could easily become 'not so nice'.

"Hi mate, nice to meet you." All these faces had at one time been connected to the Firm, or still were connected one way or another and were kept at bay by Johnny the hit man. Only a small few were closely connected to Mr Nice even though they had worked in the same Firm as well as looking after their own smaller Firms.

The ones that weren't so close were now on the run or would soon be going down themselves. The police were onto them and that's why Malcolm was here; to tell them. They were now on their own and Mr Nice was cutting his ties with all of them … It was nothing personal; it just pays to be safe in his eyes. The less people around him the better. They were wanted and the police were asking too many questions.

Soon after, some other villains joined us at the table. These too would soon be caught for whatever they had been doing. That's if they weren't already on bail or being watched, or on the run. It's a small world out there in the underworld. It seems that somewhere along the line everyone has done a bit of work for someone or other. No matter how low down the ladder they may seem to be. Even those that were at the top of the game. Some of them still owed one another favours for work carried out before the funeral.

It's weird as now all this had happened even sworn enemies amongst the Firms had joined forces and forgotten all about their differences, anything to try and get away from the police. Now, the pound note seemed to be mightier than the sword. Things were being put down on paper and were being published. They were making money in other ways; with guest appearances, films and books, and they had forgotten all about what had happened in the past, including their differences with rivals.

They were in the limelight, it was best they didn't get deeply involved with the other members of the Firms that were still at large. One of the villains that were sat there with us, next to the two bare-knuckle fighters Aggie and Manny C had walked into the Manager's office. Andy asked me to go in there too, and he introduced me to the Manager. We had a few lines and he said,

"Stay here for a bit," as he was waiting on the phone for the other fella. He said, "Look, we'll get it sorted for him, just tell him that."

"Look, Charlie," The fella was talking on the phone loud enough for all to hear in a big thick London accent, "I told you the three of us went round there. We told him to behave himself otherwise it will get messy and will no doubt end in tears, and not only his tears but his family's as well." The geezer continued, "He said he had run the gambling machines for years and he had run this club alongside them. So, I told him the only thing he would be running from then on, if he didn't pay back the money owed to the club, would be the fucking London marathon if he had any legs left after we finished with him." Chuckling he continued his tale, "I said, 'You want the outstanding?' and he said, 'Because you're away he thinks he doesn't have to pay it back. He says you're never going to be let out, so you will never need it.' He only has the front to pull a fucking shot out on me and say to tell you that the money is coming in slowly and he will pay you when he has it or if you get out on parole. He says you don't need it in a hurry stuck in there. Then he has the front to say to me that he doesn't want me or my missus, that Shirley tart, in his club again cause we're not welcome …"'"

Loving the sound of his own voice, "He even said 'Look gentlemen, I'll pay you half of what I owe him and you can keep it and say it's not happening.' So, the thing they had said was they had taken the pay-off and still told Charlie he wasn't paying. He promised they would do something but had done nothing."

The fella continued speaking, "Charlie, he will not pay, and the more we do the more he will not pay as he says, 'Go on do it. You'll never see your money then will you.' So the boys instantly pulled their shooters on him and I told him, 'we're all fucking gangsters round here, and I'm not just some mug messenger. I'm here helping an old East End friend out with his interests.'"

On and on this tale twisted, "So before you start snarling at me like a dragon … the only difference between you and me is that I have got the guts to pull the trigger and watch as the content of your head splatters on the floor."

There was more, "He laughed. So I took the gun out of his hand and whacked him with it. I told him we would be back for the money or him, so he only had twenty-four hours left otherwise he was a dead man and we would put more holes in him than a fucking watering can. I saw the Bentley outside as Mr Nice drove past the club, someone had put one in his mate. So, after talking to him and thinking all was well, next thing I know, I have two blacked-out cars turning up at Shirley's flat with seven black fellas and a big lump knocking on the door. When she opened it they walked in asking Shirley where their fucking cocaine was. We knew we hadn't even got it for them. It was a blag from the prick at the club. He had only set me up and sent the hit squad round to the fucking missus' house, and you can guess the rest mate. I still haven't heard the last of it from her, she still going on about it now. 'What if the kids had been off from school?' Honestly, woman love to nag, I get this shit to boot, 'If you don't want to be involved then stay away from my home and keep your shit away from us.' So he has got to get it mate money or no money. I ain't buying that Charlie; he mugged me right off."

He paused while Charlie spoke on the other end of the line.

"Old Friend of yours or not, mistake or no mistake, 'cause you're banged up he's taking your kindness for a weakness Charlie. Coming on a visit and paying your uncle a thousand pounds when he owes you fifty thousand? What I want to know is this, who's more dangerous, this gangster or his fucking runners? Whichever one Charlie you have my word it will get sorted whether you like it or not mate. If they come to my house again it will get sorted one way or another."

Charlie said something in reply.

"You know how it is Charlie; you don't go round the missus' house. You come see me face to face."

Then it went quiet.

"Look, Charlie, whether they come from Liverpool, Manchester or whether they're all flesh and guts, we've all got names. I have a phone full of them, but I would rather do my own dirty work. You get more respect that way in this underground world we move in. It's always been about respect and that's my currency. If you don't have respect then you're going nowhere fast. As you know, respect is everything Charlie."

It went quiet again, and then he continued;

"Look, I don't care who he is, as Smith and Weston have

143

done a big favour for mankind. He has made all men equal. So fuck the lot of them, well, if they come near Shirley's flat again then, well you know the rest Charlie and how it ends even if he's related to you or not. So save the top bunk for me. I could be coming in soon."

He listened as Charlie spoke again.

"Yes. The security has been sorted out for the funeral mate Big D is doing it. Don't worry, there was a little bit of banter about who was to do it, but he was told being a gangster isn't about looking tough, but it's all ready and will be all nice and amicable. Everything will be done for your brother, you have my word."

Another pause on the line a few choice uh huh's a hems and then, "So, your pal with the money for the club. He really does need to be educated in the ways of the Firm. You leant him the money to get his business off the ground and all he has paid back is a monkey, now that's a liberty in my book Charlie. That's cheeky."

Becoming increasingly animated, face contorted with passion he went on, "Look, let me tell you, I'm scared of no man mate. Names don't scare me as we're all blood and guts, or haven't you noticed? I know you have been banged-up for some time now Charlie, but things are changing, and changing fast in London. My friend in the East End keeps telling me it ain't the same as it was thirty years ago and let me tell you mate, he's right. It's different from when you and your brother were here. This world is full of wrongs mate and I'm doing the world a favour by getting rid of another one. If he tries it again he is a dead man, one word to Mr Nice and you know the rest. People seem to forget that the gangster's runner is more dangerous than the gangster himself Charlie. I'll just let them both have it. Funny thing is they won't even know where or who it came from. I'll be in touch Charlie. As you say, it's forty five grand."

On the other end of the phone Charlie spoke for a few minutes while the fella nodded.

"Okay, Charlie, it's a deal my friend. You know I won't fuck about. As a matter of fact, I'm here now with the boys. We're just having a friendly meet as Johnny was killed by the police a week ago so I can't get him to do it... Mr Nice has sent his new number one, Malcolm, so we can all get acquainted."

I leant in closer so I could hear Charlie's side of the conversation.

"Just, do as I ask and get the money back for me. The bitch that runs his accounts keeps saying she will go to the police if anything happens to him. Sort her out too, I hate being blackmailed. Even more so when I'm stuck in here."

"Okay, well I'll put the feelers out for them and her."

"Yes, you do that."

"For fuck sake Charlie, stop flapping. We'll get it sorted. I'll grab a few faces and we'll go and pay him another visit. I'll get one of them to tell her to keep her mouth shut about fretting with the police all the time. The little slut! They're all the same them fucking cocaine hags. You can always rely on them to fuck things up mate."

"Look I know."

"If she keeps talking then we'll have to hold her down and staple it shut for her. Okay mate. I'll be up to see you at the weekend. We'll talk some more then."

The fella stopped talking and placed the phone down and started talking to one of the Old Boys in the office.

"Did you get the money for Charlie then?"

"Yes," he said as he opened the safe and pulled it out, "Here, half for us and half for you Andy. Just say you have sent men round there and he has been sorted if ever asked."

"Will do."

We then had another line before we left the office and sat back at the table.

Vivian wasn't paying any notice to the whole thing. They seemed to buzz off the danger of it all. Vivian was having none of it. To her, it was all bollocks and she was just there for a good night out at the club. All this gangster stuff; names and villainy, talk and bravado, was just stupid, to her and she wasn't impressed or being blinded by it one bit. Money, drugs and violence didn't impress her at all. She knew what it looked like from the outside and it wasn't all it was cracked up to be. She knew a lot of people had to get hurt and she didn't like that one bit, or the money that came from these things. To her, family and principles were enough. They were worth much more than any money or respect a drug dealer or gangster could make or get.

A few of them had let their principles go and were now all out for themselves. They didn't care who they had to hurt to get to where they wanted to be. She just wanted me to be out of it and to not be a part of it in any shape or form, as soon as possible.

I, however, felt a sense of belonging with the Firm. James T, a stocky fella, about 5ft 7, and a right true Londoner also sat at our table that we had been invited to sit at while we waited for Old School to arrive. He was, very loud and he talked in a real deep voice. Someone had said he was linked to some of the missing gold that had been robbed, but no one knew for sure. James T was also a thug and a football hooligan. He was wanted for murder. He had been involved in a drive-by shooting on another gangland connection that had threatened his family over the whereabouts of

146

some stolen gold from the brinks 'allegedly.'

He was the one that was on the phone to his mate Charlie K who was at the time banged up with his brother and his other brother who had died, and they had asked his Firm to sort out the security for the funeral. He had a little trouble with a rival family off the Old Kent Road. He was also wanted for ABH, as he had kicked (nearly to death) a rival fan outside a football game whilst the poor fella was taking a piss in the hedge. He had jumped him while the other fans had smashed the poor fella to bits. Then he pushed him into the water where the fella drowned because he was too injured to swim.

I hate bullies and I didn't like him one bit. He was too loud and flash for my liking. Then there was Alan F, who was a major drug kingpin. He too had shot dead his drug seller outside a gym in Tenerife because of overdue drug debts. Some say it was over some steroids deal they were involved with. It was a case of he had just wiped his mouth of the money owed. He didn't want to listen to his bollocks anymore and when Alan F asked him for the money owed, he told him; "Look mate, I don't have all of it so you're just going to have to get in line like the rest of them." That was the last straw for Alan. He couldn't believe he had the audacity or the balls to speak to him like that. As big of a body builder he was, the steroids had gone to his head and he was suffering with rage. Alan F had been waiting for him in the gym toilet and then put a 9mm bullet in the back of his nut, killing him instantly as he walked into the gym showers.

Once he heard the shower going. Alan F had come out of the toilet and as the fella was showering, had put the Lucozade bottle on the end of the gun, then on his head. As he wiped the soap out of his eyes to see what was going on.

Alan F pulled the trigger, leaving the big muscle blown lump slumped up in the shower. The bigger they are, the harder they fall, and he had made sure of that. He had dropped the gun into this fella's sports bag, wiped it over with the tail and then slipped out the fire exit he had come through.

After the shooting Alan F had come over to England to lay low for a bit. He was a slim-built fella, around 5 ft. 8 with black hair and a tattoo of a saint on his left arm. His right wrist had a swallow on it. He wore a fat Rolex watch and yes, this was a real one and not a fake. I watched the hand hover around as I looked at him as he swigged at his Jack D's. He had a big connection with these Asian fellas who were bringing in steroids, and he knew loads of body-builders and gyms to sell them to. He was making a killing out in Tenerife until the situation in the gym loo went down.

Here we were sat with killers and I sat studying the man in front of me, making my own presumptions about him … His missus he had brought with him was a major villainess herself. She owned a few Escort agencies in Hampstead and was making a lot of money. She was once married to a wealthy landlord and was now running her own swingers' clubs. I took everyone at face value and didn't listen to the talk about this man and that. Once the police had caught up with these men they would most definitely be getting kilted off, but at the moment, they were all living as fugitives on the run, or under the cover of aliases.

They were trying to keep a low profile now that the police had photos of them from the funeral. It was silly of them being there really, putting themselves on offer, but they were paying respect and showing loyalty to Johnny, in their eyes it was the right thing to do. This whole life-style was about taking risks. I could see why Mr Nice wanted to distance himself from them and just have a few hand-picked fellas close. They were all staying as low as they could whilst on the run and in hiding. However, they had risked it a little by coming to the club this night for this last meeting. Well, they had all had a hand in the money they were supposedly giving back to him so they were there also for that. They also, wanted to hear what Malcolm was going to say to them. Well the club was run by the Firm's people now so it was still a low key club, even though it was still open to the public.

It's amazing how you see people but can't remember seeing them, if you know what I mean. Old School and Malcolm hadn't met before but they were to meet a few seconds before he came to pass the info to everyone. He had told us that Mr Nice would be away soon trying to sort out a cocaine deal again as the other deal had gone wrong, or that's what he had led us all to believe. He said he would let them know once things were all sorted and in place and running like clockwork. Then they could all get back to work and have a share of the pie once the cocaine started to come over and an agreement could be made.

It was a blag, just to get out there and see if anyone found out he was asking for Mr B's number . This was also a bid to sweeten them up so they would do as they were told and they were all falling for it. He then left after he had told them that those who were on the run or known were no longer welcome in the Firm and that they should from now on cut all ties. As if they were known they were now a liability as they would no doubt be followed by the police or would have an investigation pending.

Malcolm told them all that trying to talk to everyone on

the phone would have been too hot and easier for the police to link everyone together. So, if they were to start working on the cocaine that Mr Nice said he was now working on, then they would have to stay away and meet up at a place they all knew. They were not to use the phones anymore.

Then there was Keith, who was sat at the table too. Keith was wanted by the police for a violent attack on a door staff member and a club owner. The club we were now sitting in, and it was now our doormen working there and protecting it, or at least who had control of it after this little incident they had told me about. Apparently, it was so bad that the aftershave man was told to get in the toilet, shut the door and shut up or he would get it too. They told him this as they frogmarched the manager into the toilets. So, he had been told to shut himself in the toilet cubicle next to where Keith was smashing the manager about. The aftershave man had fallen on his knees while listening to the Manager mumbling to himself "Please, please," as he could hear the club manger begging for his life and begging the aftershave man to help him out. He heard the fist with the knuckle duster on it raining down on the manager with each squeal of pain. He couldn't help as he would have been confronted by the gun man that told him to be a good lad and shut the door or he would be next, but don't worry; you'll get a big tip for cleaning this crap up.

"Please! Look, please! I'm sorry. I didn't know she was sixteen for crying out loud. She looks twenty-two. Help me! Help me!" And after a shriek, it all went silent. Then a thud. It was said that he had tried it on with a Face's daughter who had paid them to sort the club manager out as one night of sex had got her knocked up.

The club manager had invited her and her friend into

150

his office and after a sniff of the shiny berliny (Cocaine) he touched her leg and she kissed him. Her friend saw what happened and when he cuddled up to her too, she pushed him off and went out of the room then when her friend had come looking, she caught the manger and the young girl having sex. She left her friend and told her mate's dad what had happened. The other girl he had put his arm around was only sixteen but to be fair she did look about twenty to twenty-one when she wore make-up and they had to be eighteen to enter the club. Her dad was a Face and when he heard about this he told the boys and they said 'consider it done'. Money was exchanged and they paid the manager a visit.

The aftershave man was on his knees as a pool of blood trickled under the cubicle door to where he sat. After the attack, Keith opened the door, sprayed himself with aftershave, pulled his clothes together and flicked a pound coin in the bowl. He picked up a chewing gum and a lolly, opened it and stuck it in his mouth. Then he passed the chewing gum to Johnny the hit man who was outside the aftershave man's toilet. He then pushed the toilet door open and said, "Here," as he pushed a fifty pound note into his top pocket,

"Clean this shit up will you?" He said as he walked out and into the club with Johnny. They walked off with these two women that had been waiting for them outside after they had seen them coming in from the dance floor.

"You were taking ages in there," one of the women said.

"Yes Darling, I was taking a shit," said Keith glibly.

"Ugh, you dirty basted," she laughed.

"You'd better believe it darling."

The women looked at each other and then at Johnny.

"Well, if you think that's dirty wait tell I get you home."

They both laughed.

Then there was David A. He was very connected in Liverpool and to their underworld. He was a fella well connected to the bands. He was very good friends with a customs officer who I had met once in Dover when Mr B had told me to meet the Liverpool fella at Knightsbridge. I had driven down in the Japanese car with a case full of cash and then I had driven back in an empty red sports car, which I now know was imported just for the job by Wong. Unknown to me, it had also been packed up with cocaine and was the easiest car to strip and pack up with drugs.

David and the customs officer had served in the army together and had done their service in Ireland. David had saved his life whilst out there serving in Northern Ireland. They had become thick as thieves.

It was this David that had introduced Mr B to the Liverpool mob and the other Firm they worked with and in turn he had introduced them to the aforementioned customs officer for a little cheque every time a shipment went through. This David, already knew Malcolm as they once owned a fruit and veg stall on Kilburn High Road when they were younger-small world heh!

That's how Malcolm got to meet the customs officer, but he wasn't involved then. However, he knew what he was all about now but didn't let on to the Firm he knew when he had been brought in by Mr Nice. As, he had also been on a meeting just by being in David's car at the wrong time while they talked about villainous circumstances. David A was now the owner of a few fish and chip shops scattered around London, and someone said he owned a few newspaper stands before they had been bought out by the Evening Standard. His brother, Clark Wilson, was also a

Gunsmith who used to convert Mac 10 Machine guns back into lethal weapons. They can spray anything they are fired at with a thousand bullets per minute at a cost of only five hundred to eight hundred pounds a pop and this could be done in his garden shed.

Andy A would then sell them on to criminals and to the Faces of the underworld and also keep a few around him for use in a time of need. Sometimes the weapons would get into the wrong hands and be passed on to thugs in street gangs and teenagers, one of whom was arrested on a routine stop and search by the police when they found a Mac 10 in the boot of his car and a hand-gun in his girlfriend's bag.

They were delivering them to another street gang in South London when they had been stopped pulling out of a well-known rough estate in London. She had crumbled and then blabbed where he had first got them from. So armed response were soon at Dave's brother's house holding everyone at gun point and arresting him. The rest of the family said they had no idea what he was doing in the shed and they were very shocked indeed.

So, that gig and drugs had helped Andy to fund a lot of things that had gone down in and around the underworld. You didn't argue with a man who had a brother with that kind of fire power at arm's reach, and that's why he was Mr Nice's friend and had been very close to Andy B. He was one of Johnny's very good pals too, as every trigger man needs a gunsmith to take care of his weapons from time to time.

He had a fat Cartier watch on his wrist and was a little stocky. He had well-chiselled looking features and was a bit of a brute. He also wore a diamond ring, made of silver or platinum. He looked a little like Desperate Dan out of the comic. As I was about to leave with Vivian, Old School finally turned up. Malcolm was just leaving too.

"About time mate."

"You know how it is Cookster."

"Where you going son?"

We were interrupted by Malcolm.

"Hi, I take it you're Old School. I have heard a lot about you, Mr Nice speaks highly of you …" They looked at each other and then Old School spoke.

"Women want me and men want to be me. So, who wants to know?"

"Look, I'm Malcolm, Mr Nice's Mate. I'm sure the boys will fill you in with what's what. I don't want to repeat myself as I have to get going now. I need to make a trip to Liverpool. David, I hope you will come with me and introduce me to the Firm and what's what up there. Also, that's why I asked everyone to be here on time. So I could clue you all up on the bad news about Johnny."

"Okay Malcolm." Old School looked at him for a split second and said, "I already know about Johnny." As Malcolm turned and disappeared through the crowd he muttered to Andy B,

"There's something about him I don't like mate."

Old School sat down.

"Where are you going Cookster?" He asked me as I was getting up.

"It's getting late and I am a bit tired so I want to go home mate."

Vivian had come back from the ladies' and wanted to leave early, and I'm glad she did as it would have been another heavy night with Jack Daniels and plenty of hard sniffing at the devils dandruff as one line is never enough and a thousand is always far too many.

"I have brought an eighth of cocaine with me. Take her home and come back, or just sit down son and I'll have a few pole dancers coming soon. And I'll get a driver to take her home."

Viv flashed me one of her *don't even think about letting me down* looks, "Come on let's go."

"Not for me Old School, I'm off home."

"Okay mate. I'll ring you once I hear from Mr Nice again."

"Okay."

"I'll let you know what the crack is mate."

"Okay."

Old School turned up with Noel C who had escaped from prison with the help of a female officer. He was shagging her before he got banged up again for a few months. She would bring him phones and some puff now and then in side Pintail prison. She helped him to escape, but he broken both his ankles once he had jumped the prison fence.

The travellers were outside waiting for him in a van. They got him and they were gone. Once his ankles were better, he had got involved with another Firm and was now wanted for conspiring to steal 1.25 million pounds from security at Heathrow airport. They were also wanted on a series ram raids all over the UK.

His little travelling Firm were all 'Career Criminals' that would help other criminals with money they had made from their little car-running scams. They stole cars and performed robberies, and they used the money to buy and sell drugs. The travellers had been caught on a job trying to steal some metal from a warehouse, but he got away with it.

Noel C was the one that helped the jewellery thieves organise the robbery from prison, and the money was shared out at the time when we were all at the party which was laid on at the History for the Jewellery thieves release from prison. It was at this party that I first met Mandy, God rest her soul. How else were they going to pay for it after just coming out? The jewellery thieves had planned the robbery for them whilst in prison and they had executed the plans for them on their release of Mr Adam and that's when I first met Mr Nice.

I had met them at the History night club. That's where the money was shared out amongst us all being present that night. Next to Old School stood two bare-knuckle fighters, about seventeen stone of muscle each and both they were both boxers. One of them that sat at the table was Manny C, and next to him was Aggie, who was now coming out of retirement. He had hung his gloves up for a while but was now back in business and wanted to fight once again at Eros night club in Enfield after three years of training and getting back into shape. He wanted to fight again to get back some money after the mugs he had around him back then had run him into the ground and left him penniless, but now he was back on the up and in with the Firm. He was ready to fight once again and in more ways than one. Once the underground fights could get sorted out again he had entered another one and had won his return fight. So things were good.

I asked Old School if he had heard anything from Mr Nice.

"No, nothing more mate, only what you know already. Only what you told me but I'm sure we will hear from him again soon. As it starts to kick in that we haven't got any money around us anymore and we aren't paying for anything we had taken off him in Spain."

"Fuck him. No news is good news son. So stop worrying. And that Malcolm I don't think he's got it in him."

He sniffed up hard. He had also been sniffing before he had arrived by the sounds of it.

"Come on, let's go …" Vivian said.

"Look, I'll see you later Old School."

"Yes Cookster, you will mate."

As I left, Dave D and Andy B were at the door.

"See you son, and if you ever want to come to my club again then just let us know. We'll make sure you have a great night. Bye sweetheart." Andy said as we left the night club.

CHAPTER 20

Mr Nice needed a break from the dramas that had gone on back in London and also from losing the field and the missing cocaine in Colombia. As you can imagine, it was a stressful situation to be in with a lot of pressure and money at stake, not to mention peoples' lives. Now, we had to get the other cocaine across the borders. He knew he now had to be out of the way as he had heard from us that Johnny had been killed by The Old Bill and that Wong and other members of the Firm had nearly got themselves nicked by being present at the cemetery at Mandy's funeral as he had arrived with him.

With that and other things that had happened and had started to crop up, meant Mr Nice needed to be out in Marbella away from it all in London. He needed to take care of a few loose ends with regards to other business matters that had arisen with a call he had got, which lead to him doing a job and then being told to meet a Mafia Don out in Puerto Buenos, but before he had done this, he had been in another part of Spain sorting out the outstanding cocaine and the cannabis coming over on the lorry. He hoped this was now on its way to another part of Spain, ready to be shipped out to London if Fritz could get it to the shipping yard ready like he said he could and had been now paid to do so.

Wong wanted a chat with Mr Nice, face to face, as certain things had started to go wrong for a business partner friend of his now Johnny was out of the way.

"Look come out to Marbella with me," said Mr Nice. "Sort out my loose ends and then I'll help you sort out you bits. Just make sure the German can do what he says he can once he meets up with Curtis. Let's make sure he gets out there to Curtis and then we can talk and see what the best way forward is for all of us. It'll be good for you to be out of London for a bit longer Wong. I'm sure Yang, your good women, will look after everything."

"She's my minder if you must know Mr Nice."

Mr Nice wanted Wong with him now Johnny was out the picture. He knew Wong could handle himself, as he was once a prize fighter in Indonesia for an underground organisation back in the day. So, Wong had come out to Spain to the shipping yard, done the business with the German fella at the other shipping yard ready to get him sorted ready to meet up with Curtis in Colombia to get things moving with the cocaine and bring it back, or at least try to think of the best way to smuggle it over from the other part of Spain.

Mr Nice, heading out to Marbella on a beautiful yacht that was now reflected in the Mediterranean Sea as it pushed forward into the clear blue water, cutting though the waves, as it got closer to the coast of Marbella, ready to dock at Puerto Buenos and meet the Mafia Don. As the yacht came near land, you could see some of the fantastic real estate of Kristina Szekelys, the most successful woman of real estate on the whole coast. It's said Kristina is the queen of Marbella society. Wong and Mr Nice had sailed over here for a well needed break and to assess the situation they now found themselves in.

"You can help me out with a little business that has cropped up." Mr Nice had said to Wong.

Mr Nice wanted Wong out in Marbella with him as a little back-up. Before they had found themselves coming out here he had got a call, out the blue, from a woman in Manchester, saying she was the wife of the Sicilian mob boss and that she wanted to meet up with him. She said it was very important they met and had a chat about Johnny, so a meeting had been arranged.

Until he knew what it was all about, Mr Nice was a little unsure of it all at and had his doubts. They met and she said that Don F wanted him to go to a Spanish villa and help dig up some money. After the meeting with her it started to make sense to him a little after being put on the spot and being asked to do this little job.

Mr Nice was told to do the job then, go over to Marbella with this money ready to see the Mafia mob boss, as he wanted a meeting with him now he was bringing the money over to him. She said he would pay him well if he had done what his wife from Manchester had asked of him.

Don F wasn't expecting it to be there. He thought that Johnny had got to it beforehand and may have already dug it up. As he couldn't contact Johnny not knowing he was, in fact dead, he was hoping that Mr Nice would do the job. Hoping the money was still there and would be on its way out to him as arranged. As he hadn't heard from Johnny since the shooting of the Bradford mob. Don F was a top enforcer out in Sicily, but it was getting hard for them too, as traders were told that they would evade local taxes if they grassed on the Mafia extortionists.

So, he had moved from the island of Base Sicily as the business had grown sick of paying protection money to his racketeers, and they had agreed to help cops nail them. Because of this he had to get out of Sicily fast and, now he had his claws in Puerto Buenos, they were raking in twenty billion a year and those who refused to pay got hurt and killed. The mayor of Ragusa said that if anyone that cooperated with the authorities to shut them down would be immune from their local taxes, so he had come out here to safeguard his interest, but it had gone a bit wrong for them too.

He had been there while a family was executed, but he wasn't involved in it but the police wanted to arrest him for it if he didn't stand witness to it, as he had seen what had happened. He was also largely behind the masterminding of the deaths of some anti-Mafia judges and the rival crime family figureheads that he was once involved with. But now out on his own he had to think fast. He probably had a contract on him, as they would have found out he was a witness in the execution, but not by his own choice, and he wasn't prepared to go down for life for it as he didn't do it and why should they be free to enjoy their life and family while he rotted in jail?

He had cut his close ties and was now a recluse and worked only with certain individuals as he knew it was only a matter of time. Don F was stuck in prison but he would soon be released but he needed a few things taken care of first before he came out as it was too risky for him to do the things he had asked Mr Nice now to do through his wife.

But the police couldn't have people taking the law in to their own hands and have more dead bodies on the street. He would have seen the whole thing and much more than the CCTV footage that police had looked over. He would have picked up the whole thing as it unfolded, making it easier for the attorneys to put a case across as he would have seen it happen at a different angle. The authorities could place Don F there all the way till the murders and after so the bits the CCTV missed. The Mafia Don would have seen and was now a key witness in the case, whether he liked it or not.

While Mr Nice was in Marbella he intended to ask Don F if he wanted some of the cocaine that was still stashed over in Colombia and if he said yes, then he may help out by getting it over for him. So, everything would be dealt with regards to the cocaine still in Colombia and soon he would be able to collect some of the outstanding payoffs that were owed by the Liverpool Firm.

It would give him time to work out what was now to happen with the rest of the sixty keys in Colombia that was stashed up ready for Fritz to get out there- as he was stalling a little for some reason even though he had now agreed to help.

What Mr Nice had now got from the villa in Spain, Don F would be waiting for and he wanted it brought to Marbella. In a few hours' time, he would be a free man again, if the police didn't give him a gate arrest to put pressure on him or take him in to custody for his own safety on their witness protection program as they wanted him for their witness for them on this high profile case.

He knew his life was also in danger, but once on police protection, he would lose millions of pounds because they would dive into his accounts. He was due to be released for the tax evasion charge and his first point of call would be this meeting with Mr Nice in the hope of collecting what was his and Johnny's from the job they had done on the Asian Firm.

Mr Nice had done what was supposed to be done. The money was now in Mr Nice's possession ready to hand back over to Don F on his release.

News travels fast in the underworld and news also travelled about Mr Nice being well involved with the Colombians, even though he now wasn't. Johnny would kill if it was necessary and that had spread around like wild fire in the underworld by two different Firms and people who were in the know within the criminal underworld's circles. Mr Nice and his Firm had now got a name for themself and a big reputation and it was all around the underworld and on lower level criminals and crook's lips. If the other Firms heard Johnny or Mr Nice's names then they knew not to mess around or take the piss and to take everything that was said as gospel.

They knew that everything was strictly business, not pleasure and they also knew that Malcolm had been made into the boss for Mr Nice so he could keep an even lower profile. The police had info on this too, but they needed facts and evidence. Now, the police knew Mr Nice also knew the heat was on him and he knew it was.

After ten years it's hard to go unnoticed in this line of work. Other Firms would use their names without us knowing to scare other low-level crooks into doing what they wanted them to do and some of the people involved were now working for the police which meant they were allowed to do these things as long as they grassed up all who were involved with them, to stop them going to prison themselves. Mr Nice had been introduced to a lot of people, which had led to more connections being made for Mr Nice to get as big as he had now become.

Before Mr Nice had done the deal for Don F, he had started to concentrate his efforts on trying to get this cocaine over with Fritz from the shipping yard, but in the meantime, he had met up at Johnny's bar with a few marines that were drinking there. The Father of one of the Marines called Zack Brady wanted to buy the bar. He was a property investor and thought it would be good to build villas on the plot of land that Johnny's bar currently occupied.

Mr Nice was now ready for the German to come out and meet Curtis to sort out how they would move the cocaine and for his men to receive it. While this was all done, Mr Nice would be sitting all nice and cosy, far away in Johnny's bar with Wong, drinking in front of many witnesses so he had an alibi ready for when they did come and try to arrest him for his involvement, if it went wrong.

Losing the field was a big setback for Mr Nice. He had gone to Barbados and started drinking in the local bars and in time he had made friends with a few Americans, one of whom was the aforementioned Zack Brady. His son, Brett who ironically was a marine that was attached to HMS Drug Stoker. How's your luck?

Brett and his team worked hard and played hard. They liked to party hard and liked the casinos and a few local women and a few E's as they had told Mr Nice. Ironically enough, they were patrolling the waters for drug trafficking.

So, Mr Nice thought if *you can't beat the enemy then join the enemy*. Sensing a new angle developing here, he cultivated a relationship with Brett. Mr Nice was not in the market for flogging the bar at this time, as he needed the bar to be turning money over for him and to use to put the dirty cash through. With all the mega deals lined up, this would become increasingly important.

However, Mr Nice was very interested in Brett and so to keep things sweet between them, Mr Nice said he may sell it once all his other business deals came to pass as he knew how much it would be worth to the struggling American developer.

Brett and his buddies kept blowing a lot of money on cards and the fast life while they were on leave, and they had now been corrupted by Mr Nice. Brett had become a bit crooked as money in whatever currency, in whatever country, can speak a thousand languages in this game and now he had lost a lot on the card games, he was struggling more than ever.

Mr Nice said that he had heard there was a lot of corruption going on in the forces as it seems there have been a lot of back-handers being handed over by drug cartels and that bodyguards were also taking back-handers and other bits and bobs to turn a blind eye.

"Well funny you should say that ..." Brett said to Mr Nice. He told him that he had stumbled on one of his colleague's computers whilst working on the Navy ship and that he had accidently opened a file that was marked 'top secret', thinking it was the one that was for him ready to brief his crew for their next assignment. He had accidently clicked on the file, it opened, and it had contained over 100 images of wrens that had been naked in the show on the boat they were serving on; HMS Drug Stoker.

The ship was patrolling the Caribbean waters to stop drug trafficking coming across. The photos had also shown them all getting high and there was also a sex video on there of one of the two wrens and four guys, which was being sold to others on a downloading site.

As he had looked at it more and more, he noticed that the camera that had taken the photos was on the same ship they were on board and must have been placed in a cut out hole in the wrens' changing rooms, or other rooms the wrens used. The marine managed to identify the man responsible for the recordings, as he could see his name on the files within the folder.

It was only one of his landing team. There were also photos on there of them taking drugs and having sex with one of the wrens in the shower. The camera had accidently filmed the person who had put the camera there, as his own image was caught in the mirror slightly and it had only turned out to be the Captain's son.

Mr Nice couldn't believe what he was hearing. He had also said that most of the crew were taking E's and cocaine on the boat now and that he himself had got one of the wrens pregnant while they were partying but no one knew yet as she had not begun to show. If anyone found out, then they would all be in trouble as it's all been all kept hush hush until they can work this one out and get off HMS Drug Stoker.

"We were going to confront the Captain about what we had seen and see if we could get a new team out here. Then we can get off till she has the baby. That's the plan."

"What?" Mr Nice said. "No way, you're shitting me son. Things like this don't go on, do they?"

"I'm being deadly serious."

Curtis had rung his dad and told him that he was going to sail some of the cocaine over but was in talks with the German fella and that it was still there and things seemed okay for now. He asked if he could send some more money over using Western Union because he was running low.

Mr Nice said he would send some money over and was glad things were now working out.

"The pervert taking the photos and filming the wrens is only the Captain's son. Who is also serving on the same ship as me," Brett continued, "So, once I saw one of my landing crew shagging in the showers with one of the wrens I had to do it. I put in a disc and downloaded the images and as it was downloading, there it was, a two minute film of the Captain's son and another officer at it."

"Two men?"

"It was disgusting, and I turned the monitor off and stopped downloading. I wanted to shoot the fella."

Then he said he had turned it on again once he had downloaded.

"I placed it in my uniform and then left. The next day he was on land, which is where I have met you with my dad. I know he is really interested in buying Johnny's Bar from you as the other deals he has had have gone pear-shaped and he has lost a lot of money in the recession. He has had others pull out at the last minute as they too have lost a lot of money with the state of the economy and investments they had had in Iceland and Dubai. He knows the Villas will be a great investment if he can do the deal with you."

Brett divulged all of this, not knowing what Mr Nice was really all about. He just thought he was a shrewd businessman. Well, he was, but in the narcotics game not properties.

He said he was the head landing parting officer that would board the ships to confiscate the cargo and arrest the occupants on board. The stuff they would normally find on-board the ships was drugs or contraband and sometimes arms and occasionally money.

"We would take a little bit for ourselves and party with the wrens and the other crew on board."

Mr Nice was very interested in this and within time they had become good friends and he had introduced him to his pal who owned the card place with the strip girls. The strip girls had partied with them and had got him very drunk and they sniffed cocaine and taken E's and while this had gone on Mr Nice had taken the disc and copied it for himself. The girls had given him E's and they had all partied hard one night back at a club.

So Mr Nice had a plan.

"This disc you have will be worth loads of money if you sold it to the papers."

"But it would get me in trouble too dude."

It was Mr Nice's reassurance that if anything came on top for his mate and also about the pregnancy then he would pull this out to the Captain to pull the strings to help them out.

"Look, I think you and I could make a lot of money, and I mean a lot more than you'll ever earn in your life doing what you're doing. If you do what I'm going to ask you, it would be a massive start to your lady wren with the baby. It would be a nice little earner for all of us involved and your dad will benefit from it too."

Brett was quite inquisitive at first and wanted to know more.

"How's that possible?"

"Well you could work with me."

"My Dad said you're a very ruthless businessman."

"That's right, I am. So do you want to earn some big money in a very short time?"

"How?"

Mr Nice wanted to know if he was willing to take part in the plan he had. He told him what he was all about. Mr Nice then said he would give him a share of all the profits made. Mr Nice said, "What we can do is; for every confiscation you make, you can drop half back in to the water and I'll get my son to pick it back up. Then we can split the money."

"I can't do that."

"Okay then I'm finished talking with you. I can see I'm wasting your time and more importantly mine and as you know there is a lot of money to be made from this. If I sell the bar to your dad he will make a lot of money once he develops it to Villas. That will pull him out the shit would it not with his financial decline and things? But I would be careful who you tell about you and the crew in the future and about the wren you fucked who is now pregnant and I take it was while she was on your military exercise. If they found out I'm sure you would be relieved of your duties and get busted too, disc or no disc. I have heard that anyone that falls short of their high standards could be dismissed and that wouldn't make your father proud would it? But if you don't want to make money I understand."

"How much can be made?"

"Quite a lot, maybe more then you could earn in a lifetime and no one would have to know what we are doing or how we are doing it. As long as you're seen to be doing the correct thing then all is well and good."

"Sorry, mate, no deal. I think I would rather dig myself out of my own hole."

"Well son if you don't want to, now that I have told you a little about me you leave me no option but to blow the lid on what you have just told me about to your dad and to the M.O.D. I'll have to tell them what you and your team and crew are really doing, which is getting high and the other things going on that are untoward on the ship you are serving. I'm sure the M.O.D would have a lot of explaining to do when reading about it first hand in the papers! As you said yourself, you like the odd E and cocaine now and then on leave parties and while you're over in Amsterdam. Let me quote what you just said. 'You work hard so I guess you play hard too'. The Ministry of Defence would be in uproar if they heard what you have just told me son on a whole shipload so sailors aboard a ship getting high while they should be intersecting boats themselves. That wouldn't be a good day for the Navy son, would it?"

"Well it's lucky you have no proof."

Mr Nice then played it back to him on his laptop from the wire he was wearing.

"Shit!"

"Yes shit indeed. So if you don't want to be court marshalled and your dad to find out that his marine son has knocked up a wren and does E's and cocaine on a ship supposedly trying to stop drugs coming over. Then I guess we have a deal. I'm sure you will work with me as I'm sure if he heard this it will make him really proud of you abusing your position and trust. I guess you'll now do what I want you to and will retire in a year or so; you, me and your dad. Otherwise I think you may be fast-tracked out of the marines my son and be peeling chips in some glass house. Your dad will be over the moon as you'll both have enough money to retire on without any more failed investments. You can then take your pregnant wren and retire somewhere nice and hot and forget all about it while my son speedboats to locations where you drop the stuff. If you do, you'll have a nice nest egg and I will walk away and you'll never hear from me again."

Totally stuck between a rock and a fucking hard place, Brett agreed. He explained that he would have to split his half of the money made with his team of five and he knew they would all be up for it. They were very loyal and had served most of their lives under him. He knew a few of them had also dabbled in things that were above and beyond the call of duty. They all had been taking drugs and had all been partying and getting off their nuts shagging the wrens while serving on the HMS Drug Stoker.

Mr Nice had now corrupted this marine and couldn't believe he had accepted the offer to help him out. So once on board HMS Drug Stoker Brett had asked the Captain after their briefing if he could have a chat alone.

"Yes come in. At ease." So he had entered the office. "Sit down."

"No thanks."

"So, what can I help you with? Is there a problem with the briefing?"

"No sir."

Brett calmly explained what he had found out about all the crew on board, he said they were now getting high on E's and amphetamines and shagging each other. The Captain was a bit shocked and said he would go to the top brass and thanked him for the info and said he would put enquiries out to catch all those involved and that he would look in to all allegations made. But Brett was just warming up.

"Look, there is also footage of you sleeping with a wren, but that's not important. There is more Sir."

He also told him what he had found his son doing and that it was common knowledge between the crew and that why they were freely doing what they were doing. The Captain knew his son was finished and so would also be up for allowing such things to go on aboard his ship. He would be dishonoured by his son's actions and by letting the crew get like this on his own ship. He would be the mockery of the Navy. This would ruin him and his reputation amongst his comrades. He had asked Brett how they could work things out while he made things right again.

"Shall I can give you leave if you want while I sort this mess out? We can say it's on medical grounds."

"This is what we can do, they will drop half the drugs back in the water or whatever the cargo is and then a friend of mine will collect them" Brett said, "My boarding team will do this with every boat now intercepted by HMS Drug Stoker until leave.."

"Okay," the Captain said, "We can make a report as normal with regards to the confiscation of these ships and turn a blind eye to everything else. You can then get your friend deployed. Then sort out the crew on board once me and Tara have also left on medical grounds, then everything will be okay and no one will know it ever happened or what went on."

The Captain visibly shrunk, his whole world had imploded, Brett continued, "We would return with half the drugs seized off the boats and the crooks on board. Once these things are done for five months and I deploy, then I will turn a blind eye to everything else going on this ship as they have no concern to me and you can have this folder with the photos and the disc in it. We could and would give you a drink from it and we would forget all about this little chat. You'll have all the info you need and can set up a drugs test before everyone comes on the ship once I have been deployed."

He knew he had him by his balls. The Captain just sat there considering his options. He held his glass and stared at the folder, then he opened and closed it as his eye glanced at the photos on top. Sighing heavily, he simply shrugged, "Okay."

So, on the first interception, the HMS Drug Stoker stopped a little fishing boat who was not responding to their commands. The HMS Drug Stoker had opened fire with some warning shots around the boat, but still no response from the boat or any of the crew.

The boat looked empty through the Captain's binoculars. The marines were then given the order to board the boat. So, they had dropped their boarding boat with the five marines into the water and had intercepted the boat. Once the marines were on board the fishing boat they found only one member of crew aboard. The others had jumped ship and swam for it as soon as they had seen HMS Drug Stoker.

From way back far as they knew they would be stopped and they would catch them as the boats engines had trouble. So, they were unable to get out of there. The one still on board couldn't swim which meant he had no choice but to stay on board. He desperately tried to hide himself in the hull of the boat.

He was found and arrested at gun point. Then their boat was searched. The marines had stumbled on a half-tonne of cannabis that they were trying to smuggle over. Fifty keys were then dropped back into the water without anyone else knowing on board HMS Drug Stoker and the boat and the crew members were then taken back to HMS Drug Stoker.

They had towed the fishing boat back to land and had

stayed there for three days before it was due to go on sail again. Mr Nice was given the maps with the co-ordinates on them where the fifty keys of puff had been dropped into the water, ready for Cutis to collect.

Mr Nice had been in talks with Fritz and had organised a boat for his son and a few crew to sail ten keys of the cocaine to England, and they had agreed to go to the maps co-ordinates and collect the puff on the way round.

In return Mr Nice said,

"Once my son sails it to Spain, then we'll all get paid Okay."

"Once sold?"

"Yes."

Mr Nice would get the card owner of the casino to pay Brett out in chips as he arrived. So, things would look normal and above board. He would then play a few hands and then hand the chips in to the cashier to exchange for money, no questions asked. He would then share it all with his crew and the Captain without anyone knowing apart from themselves.

It was a great set up for now, till one of the wrens failed a random drugs test and had blown it for everyone. She looked a bit off her nut at a club and was seen by two commanding officers as she left stumbling around and the admiral at the port in Portsmouth. The police had told the captain of HMS Drug Stoker that one of his crew, she in particular, had seen her looking untoward and indulging in an inappropriate behaviour and therefore was summoned to have her urine tested in the morning if they were to sail again, which they were.

The test came back positive to drugs and that's when she confessed that she and half the crew on HMS Drug

Stoker were on drugs or had taken them.

This had sparked off a massive enquiry, which ended with a series of most of the crew getting court marshalled. She had also blown the lid on Mr Nice's son as she was shagging one of the leading party and she also told them about what they were doing and that it was Mr Nice's son picking up the drugs that had been dropped by the main marine and that he would then sail it on to Spain. So, on his next drop, Curtis was caught but it wasn't cannabis this time, it was cocaine.

They caught him on board with the five keys he had tried to get to Spain. The German now needed to think again on how he was going to get the cocaine from Columbia to Spain. Mr Nice's son was sentaced to seven years for his part in the drug smuggling operation. He. When the admiral investigated more on the ship he had found that the captain's son was taking photos of the naked wrens and selling them on porn web sites. The son had come clean to his dad the captain to save himself, he then confessed about the set up with regards to the marine team and that they were intercepting the drugs.

They then set up a trap for the next shipment, which had caught Mr Nice's son. News had hit the papers that the crew of HMS Drug stoker had been court marshalled, well fifty per cent of them had.

Mr Nice still had forty keys of cocaine stashed in the old light aircraft hangar in Colombia and now had a load of cannabis too stashed in Spain in a lorry ready to be moved, but the police and Customs and Excise had his son Curtis.

He knew it would only be a matter of time before it came on top for him if he wasn't smart. So, he thought it best he stopped getting involved and let everyone else do what they had been instructed. Mr Nice pulled a fast one on us and on the Colombian Don. The aircraft hangar was camouflaged by trees and overgrown bushes. Mr Nice knew it was no good having forty keys of cocaine just sitting there hidden away and the German man should move fast but the only way to do it was to find a buyer straight away.

Mr Nice needed to be a little smarter now and would have to go it alone for a bit, at least until he could find some connections on the other side of the fence to get rid of all this lot. This is where Malcolm came in, having no one to sell it to left it just sitting there. Until Malcolm found a buyer in Liverpool for it all or for at least for forty keys more as they had already wanted twenty, but that had gone missing.

So, to have forty keys just sitting in Colombia wasn't a very good idea for Mr Nice and he felt a quite under pressure. He knew he must get it out of Colombia very soon before it came on top, but the main contact he had ready for this lot had now been caught for a big fraud scam on stolen cloned credit cards in Windsor.

That had messed things up with the German as well, as the money would have funded some more transport to get the cocaine over. They had already lost a boat but had sold the plan on to some Essex gangsters, the one the Colombian pilot had parked up at Elstree. So now they had a few quid to play with again. There was no work being done just yet and the cocaine was just sat there till Mr Nice had talked about it to Malcolm who had said he had a buyer for twenty keys.

"Who's the contact Malcolm?"

"It's the Liverpool mob. They want twenty keys first then twenty from then on every month."

The rest had been smuggled over to Spain by Mr Nice's German friend now so things were on the up. He had gotten a lorry to take the rest to a shipping yard with a convoy of Land Rovers but that was done a bit later on. The pilot had already lost the first twenty keys of cocaine on the first flight out to England. Mr Nice had tried to move some of this cocaine to Malcolm but the pilot had messed it all up as it had gone missing on the first drop as we know he had dropped it in the wrong field.

After all these mess ups and his son getting nicked, Mr Nice was very sceptical about how and with whom he was to work with to move this lot and who it would go to in the end and would he pull it off without anyone finding out that he had stolen it. So, with the pilot messing up, the cocaine just sat there in the hideout for now. The main buyer he had ready for the lot had got himself nicked in Liverpool at a club for assault. Mr Nice wanted the whole shipment moved, gone out of the way before someone told the Colombians and then he would lose the lot and his head.

If they had found out he had lied and stolen it all off them, he knew that he would get an acid bath or worse still, have his head cut off with a chainsaw and fed to the tigers; one of the two or just popped off in a drive by.

He didn't want to steal from the Colombians intentionally or off us with the money on the depot but he had seized the opportunity as it was just circumstance that had made it easier to do. He would need a big safe house in London to store this lot unless someone came up with a good idea to move the lot which he was hoping the German would. Fritz kept saying everything would be okay but he still didn't trust him, even though they had made good money from other bits they had done way back with E's from Amsterdam that he had sold to the German's brother.

He had been in talks with his friend from Brussels with

regards to moving the rest of it in to Spain ready to come over on a lorry but nothing had been sorted just yet and if it had, it was all kept quiet for now.

Mr Nice and the Sicilian mob was now willing and able to shift the cocaine he had stashed with these two top Firms help and the help of Fritz. It meant the drug trade was now booming again for him and they could all now communicate on the same friendly level and started rubbing shoulders together amicably and get the cocaine moving and over without anyone else getting killed or grassed up or having to corrupt anyone else up the ladder.

They had joined forces now with the top of the food chain and that meant work could be done and money could be made and London would be flooded once again with top gear (cocaine) around ninety-three per cent.

Mr Nice knew if they could only get it to Spain then it would come over to England in its purest form. Once it washed back, it would still be in its purest form. When it landed it would not be pressed shit with its strength kicked out of it, and would be sold on as disco dust. In the clubs and pubs and anywhere the street soldiers were selling it on to their customers, just to have a few grand in their pocket every week, while the main players were making big money once it arrived on the streets.

There was not much around at the moment. The greedy smart dealers realised that if they had a little bit of good gear they could make double the money, if not treble. If they pressed our gear once it arrived to them, all would go as smooth as planned. With Mannitol or Vide a Cain or any other stuff they could get their hands on off some university bod who was studying chemistry in their garage or some dentist that fancied a pay rise on his salary that we would provide for him for him to provide us with a good mix for us to mix it with.

Even hay fever tablets did the trick if there was nothing else around. As they were now finding out that they could get three bars of top quality cocaine that would be around ninety-three per cent and then some mantel and mixed the two together. Then press it back up for the bargain price of £25,000 a pop as it was at the time and it was still nice.

No one would know the difference. Well, only a few would know the difference and the others would be none the wiser. Some didn't care as they were still doing okay with their little set up pressed or not. They still made the same money as their cocaine was in one piece and doing the job. So why worry? They were still getting good money for it.

Their customers were getting a regular supply and still sniffing the shit that was now only costing them forty pounds a gram instead of fifty, so it was a bargain for them and all round from importer to supplier to dealer to taker; they were still all making good money.

So, to the street takers it was the real deal and they were now selling the stuff on the street and pressing it up for us and themselves. It was all okay and above board. That's when the real business could start.

It didn't matter if Mr Nice didn't have the field now. As with everything good, it soon runs out, but it had run out quicker than Mr Nice had planned. So, what he did have left needed to be rationed and that was how it was for now and that's why there was so much rubbish coke about.

Not knowing when the next lot would come over and hit the streets before the pigs got hold of it. Or the Navy would intercept the speedboats and stop it coming over the water to England. It was a bit touch and go now that the field was gone. Every bit counted and a lot of people's lives were at risk. With these new contacts Johnny and Mr Nice had made, it meant he could buy and sell from different sides of the fence and didn't need the field to conduct his growing empire.

He would buy cheap from one side of the water in Miami and sell it for more on the other side and vice versa. By him doing this it had opened up a big pathway to some of the top players in England and Amsterdam and in fact, all around the world. It kept everything looking good if the Colombians started to have doubts. Mr Nice was the man calling the shots in England and had got the nickname 'The Milkman' by his peers as he could now deliver a shipment of drugs anywhere they wanted the delivery to be.

For the right price of course. So once Wong had done his bit for the intro to the German fella and he found out that he knew Mr Nice's German friend in Prague.

Well, like I said until the field he owned got blasted and the cocaine he already had in London was running low. That's when he had to come down a peg or two. Over that side of the water as the main man in Liverpool had now been nicked too. So when the Colombians heard this they cut ties with most of it, not all villains in England and just worked with the gangsters and mobsters in Miami for a while.

Mr Nice figured that it was best to stay out of Colombian's way for good so that no one there knew his business. So, moving and living out in Spain was okay for now. It just meant the tables had turned with the two big Firms the South Americans and the Sicilian mob. As once they were getting the cocaine from his field but now he was getting the cocaine from them and had his own still sitting there waiting to be moved.

Money was coming in fast and being shipped all around the country once laundered from Wong's exchange back in London town and was then going out to Guernsey to be hidden in this business and that bank. Buried before the police and their dogs had a chance to keep up with what was really happening.

The police would be trying to catch it and catch them out by following the money on a paper trail. Or any other way they could get their mitts on it. They could then take it away by slapping a confiscation order on all their assets that were unanswerable and achieved via ill-gotten gains.

So, they could top up the police vaults and put only a small percentage back in to fighting crime. This would happen once all involved were arrested and were in front of the judge. A new law had now come out about money that you wouldn't want to travel with more than ten thousand dollars at a time; unless you could explain it or travelled without telling anyone the money was there. Before being questioned, and these questions were very irritating when stopped. As the customs would ask:

"What is the money for?" Or, "Why have you got this much with you sir?"

Even the dogs had been trained to sniff out large amounts of cash as well as the drugs and other bits and bobs.

They would ask questions you didn't like to answer or you could spark an investigation on you and the money. If they were answered incorrectly and if they weren't then guaranteed, an investigation would definitely be put on you and your accounts and more so if you were already known to the police, and you wouldn't even know about it. With fraud getting bigger and bigger every day, the fraud squad were just waiting to jump on any leads they could get, no matter how big or small.

If they got a sniff that large amounts of money was moving around or it was bent or unclean or being laundered, then they would be all over it like a rash. Criminals like and others who were working with us at the time, had to keep the money well hidden and out of the way of jealous eyes; we had to think hard before it was moved around and by whom!

Gone were the days where we bought fast cars and designer clothes and watches and expensive shoes. Everyone in the neighbourhood would now be keeping their eye on our assets and the police would be keeping an even bigger eye on our money and us and the bigger fish in the pond.

Without us knowing, just to see what sort of hands it would be ending up in and who were in fact the men at the top. Nine times out of ten, it would be other criminal hands and the main players of this game and the likes of Mr Nice, AKA 'The Milkman'. It was hard to move the money, and even harder to ship the cocaine around unnoticed, as different ways were being uncovered each time the customs had a result.

Every time they caught a load of drugs, they became more and more clued up to how it was being smuggled over. Mr Nice was still doing the lorry runs without any problems, till a lorry load of cannabis was robbed from the German friend of his, but we'll get to that story soon. A new law had been passed by federal regulations which said - if you got caught supplying drugs, the police would have the power to strip you of all your unanswerable assets and stop you going into other countries like America and Australia -.

Once you received a criminal record you could and would be banned from all the pubs and would be put on pub watch for life. This meant the landlords would be given a sheet of paper with mug shots of criminals or the dodgy or no good, and if they were seen in the pubs then the landlord would have to ask them to leave.

Otherwise the police could put pressure on them if they wanted to and would revoke their licences next time it was presented for renewal if they too didn't cooperate with them and their terms. A photo of your face would be given to every landlord in the town and you were banned for life from these boozers, even in your local boozer that you had drank in for years!

At the same time a new law had now been passed in the police forces. The power now to stop and search anything or anyone they thought was acting or looked suspicious; meaning half the population. Some of us were being pulled up every other day, because they knew what we were up to, but at that point in time, when they did pull us over, we were clean but they kept stopping us anyway in the hope we would soon get busted.

They watched known drug dealer's houses and flats that had people coming and going all night and all day long from those houses and following known drug dealers cars in the hope they would do something that they could report on.

Money and assets in this game is the hardest thing to explain in this and other criminal lines of work. There are so many people that will grass you up. Let's face it, one million pounds was spent on grasses alone last year on informants to the police. So, this year I would dread to think. If they had half the chance, crack heads, brown heads, neighbourhood watch, other crooks and even your partners and, believe it or not, the men or women you're working with just to get themselves off a charge or two.

You name them they all come out the woodwork once sitting on the big blue mat thinking about going down for a very long time. Even the fella you just hurt to pay back the tickers that he or she had run up. You can't blame them 'cause if they did grass you up they may get a cash reward. Well, some might do if they don't get a bullet in their nut. The million dollar question in the police station in the interview room would be, when you're sat there with the buzzing of the tape recorder moving round as it records every word you speak including the time and date.

"Okay. We believe your story and what you have just told us but thousands wouldn't, so I want to give you the benefit of the doubt."

"You do?"

As you smile and think you have just blagged them with your story and that you're going home sometime soon.

"So, let's say all you have told us is true."

"Yes officer it is," you reply, with a smile as big as the Cheshire cat.

"Okay. Then where did this lot come from?" They ask say dropping the bomb and wiping the smile clean of your face.

They point at the bundle of money in the evidence bag that they pull up which was seized at the raid or the stolen goods you had bought or swapped for drugs or anything you shouldn't have had on you when they had got you and now keep placing on the table in front of you.

"Well erm yes. Well that came from … erm … well my mate's dad's friend who works …"

"Save it. You know you are well and truly fucked."

No amount of bullshit or excuses is going to persuade them.

"Sorry where did it come from?" Exactly.

"So, tell us how can you afford all this when you're on the dole, you don't work and you are in a job that only pays £17,000 a year, plus you're driving around in a £8,000 car but you're still living the life of a celebrity or an Entrepreneur? You still sign on or if you're a little smarter, work."

Okay, there is near twenty thousand points in this bag, a set of scales, a shooter and half a bar of cocaine, or however much it is when you get caught and if you haven't yet. I'm sure the time will come whether it be a year or twenty years, unless you're the one in a million that do make it and retire in Tenerife or Marbella. Before you get too greedy and don't get caught. So, if you can explain that one to the police, then you're free to go. If not, it's go directly to court in the morning from the police cell or bail. As they know you're telling them a load of bollocks to try and save your arse.

If you had no answers or proof or receipts where all the money and assets came from then it was as good as gone. It would now be in the police vaults along with all your other possessions that you couldn't explain and would soon be auctioned off, if the real owners didn't come and collect it. Going, going, gone; sold to the highest bidder.

They would then go off happy as Larry, and you would be going straight back to your cell. You'll be sitting in front of the judge for your crimes, listening to him telling you your being banged up, doing time, for supplying or for anything else you might have been involved with, where your money was made by ill-gotten gains because you couldn't prove where it came from. That's why if you were smart, some if not all, of your things would have been signed over to other people and not in your name and you would pay everything with cash and not have a mobile phone and you would have a few good launderers and businesses but it was getting harder to launder money.

Even some of your friends or family could turn nasty, as some of them have done and kept the lot and given you diddly squat back. After all, it's now theirs as it's got their name all over it and you can only keep so much under your mattress yourself and so much buried in the garden and the neighbour's garden If they're not in with the police watching your every move telling them everything you're doing to get their cash reward and would see you banged up instead of telling you to sort it out.

The police are on to you and it will only be a couple of days before your nicked as they'll be raiding your house. I know the tickers have done this to avoid paying or someone gets caught with it and bubbles you up so they can keep it themselves. It's like Robin Hood. Steel from the dealer and then give to the poor, and then, tell the Sheriff. They then move on to find another dealer to buy their stuff from, leaving you to pay your main man with a list of tickers the size of an A4 sheet of paper.

Armed only with a load of excuses that he doesn't want to here. Tickers don't put money in my pocket son when you say, "Look, I have loads of IOUs." But really it's a list of you ain't getting that back from that person unless you have more gear they can run off with. Well, you may get back a ten here and there if you keep supplying them, or a few hundred, but it's always playing catch up.

Then they say "we'll come to an arrangement like I'll pay you next week," but that week never comes. As it's always next week. Next week as the ticker list grows. I was once told this little story by a dangerous villain who had loads of money hidden away in this woman's account. He had been shagging her for years, he had bought her loads of stuff and she didn't want for anything.

He ended up getting nicked for glassing someone in the face in the local pub. When it had all kicked of he had gone down for it. When he came out, the woman he was with, had now shacked up with the CID fella that had arrested him. Poor fella. If it wasn't enough to lose his missus. He now had to face her being with the copper that busted him and to top it all off, they were now sharing his house and all the villain's ill-gotten gains too.

Where is the justice in that? Well, most of the police force have got criminal records themselves so it makes you think - well some I have even met a few in side and they weren't under cover ones. What a liberty.

So, they now had a nice little nest egg courtesy of this villain to fall back on and he now had Nish and was told if he keeps harassing her he will nick him so he was left with nothing, only the clothes on his back. Well apart from a criminal record and head full of prison memories and other criminal activities he had learned about inside and their contact number.

Everything was changing and changing fast for the criminal world and the gangsters. I only met two real ones; the others were just drug dealers. Lots of faces and villains and gangsters were coming out of the nick and going straight. They were pot less now and had no choice. They couldn't get back to the skulduggery work straight away or to the level they once were. Some did, but not many unless they had been smart with their money and had a few quid buried or hidden away safely with others they trusted. A few others lucked in if the people they were working for had looked after them while inside and had a few quid for them to come out to.

Or, if they were lucky and knew someone that would lay them on some more stuff to get them on their feet again or would welcome them into their coo (crime scandals) then they would be ok. So when the day did come and they were released, the only thing some of them were coming out to into probation and a criminal record and a prostitute. If they were lucky and a fat line of Peru's finest or other drugs they couldn't wait to get their hands on to celebrate their freedom. Not fast cars and a big mansions. Well some may have. There was a camera going up now in most streets in most neighbourhoods, which were keeping an eye on everything.

The police said it was to keep the streets safe but I'm sure it was to save money and cut down on police patrols. The cameras would be keeping an eye out and watching 24/7, and more so on the no good, dodgy or anyone else connected to the criminal world that the police knew about and now had their DNA kept nicely on the home offices computers. They had been caught and were now on record and as soon as they hit the streets the camera would be buzzing around watching their every move.

Their details were also logged on the police national computers, so they were onto them and the things they would be trying to do. Once again Big Brother was on top of things. New technology was being used by the police every day, such as face and voice systems and D&A matching and vehicle plate recognition systems and very hi-tech tracker devices and other surveillance tools and cameras.

If they continued with their life of crime, it wouldn't be long before they were put back behind bars. The police would be watching them come and go from different address, here, there and everywhere like Wee Willy Winky running through the town. Now these people were being watched, it meant they were watching you too. There investigations were getting bigger, as known crooks were leading the police to other unknown crooks and on to each other without even realising they were doing it.

Kids and youths had started gangs and were dealing and making money and taking anything they could get a buzz from, and palm off as drugs. They were looking up to the old fellas and wanted the fast life; drugs, women, money, fast cars and flash clothes, champagne and clubs -they were all being blinded by the lights - just as I had been when I was younger.

They were now trying to steal their drugs too because it was far too risky to bring some over themselves. Now, those that did have it, were still trying to put the price up. Even though other drugs were coming down loads in price; like E's and speed and other drugs.

The two main contacts had now been united. They had both realised now that the drugs were a lot cheaper than when they were going through the middle man to buy them. Villains and crooks didn't need to worry so much about bringing drugs and guns over themselves when they could just rob someone that already had taken a great risk to get them over here. They couldn't go to the police once you had robbed them could they? As what would they say? *"I have just been robbed of my stash and cash and shooters."*

You'd be straight on their books. People were trying to rip each other off by selling you moody gear that had been cut for triple the price once it had been cut and pressed into blocks again. Well, there wasn't a lot coming over now. Not as much as in the eighties. So, the drugs that did come over and were here in England had to be watered down a little with something to keep the business running and the cash still coming in.

The market had opened up on the streets of London; nearly everyone or anyone was in the know and knew where they could get some sort of drug. The pink pound was booming; more and more gay clubs opened up and they loved getting off their nuts. Don't underestimate the power of the pink pound. If there weren't a lot of drugs about, whoever had some was king of the road. Drugs were the currency and those that had a steady supply, like ourselves; we were lucky to have a contact like Mr Nice. It meant they, and we, were taking over everyone else's drug business because now they were coming to us and our contacts to buy it.

Whether they liked it or not, it was supply and demand and there was a lot of demand now for cocaine because it wasn't just for the rich, it was for anyone that wanted to take it now and the last estimated info was that one in four Brits where taking cocaine or some sort of mind altering substance. There's no business without merchandise to sell now is there?

Yes you would lose one or two loads to the customs but for every two that got stopped, five or more were coming over on different routes across the water and some were even now growing their own drugs themselves in made-up flats and warehouses and garages with actinic lamps and sprayers.

While Mr Nice's Firm was bringing the cocaine over on the boats the others were getting caught on the Lorries and flights. So, once a big bust had been done on the Lorries, Mr Nice would stop the boats and use the Lorries as he knew then that the police would now be stopping the boats and not the Lorries so much.

The Triads, the Albanians, Jamaicans and Romanians and the Polish. You name them, they were all arguing amongst themselves now, shooting and stabbing each other to death, just so they could control their side of the street and the drug trafficking that was being worked on them they were even selling loads of Indian Viagra.

Even the younger kids were getting involved in drugs and the gun triad selling steroids and anything they could make a few quid on as they had grown up looking at their peers and following in the same footsteps.

They were dabbling in the devil's dandruff, cocaine and other drugs that they could sell and most of them would be carrying knives, just so they felt safe on the streets they were working on. They knew it was a concrete jungle out there and it was every man for himself now. What they didn't know was that if they carry a knife, they have more chance of being stabbed by one, if not your own knife. There were also the working women that the Polish traffickers and the Albanians had control of.

They were brought over against their own will, on the front that they would have a great new life and plenty of work that would pay well. Some of these people were connected to human trafficking in a big way and the new life they had promised these poor girls and women wasn't in some nice place where they could work with good money. It was in some old flat, prostituting themselves against their own will and being drugged up and beaten. The people who helped do this to women were pure evil.

These people were scum but they were well connected and dangerous individuals who were now well on the streets of London and other areas in Britain and abroad looking for other women and girls. Guns were being smuggled over the waters now from all the war zones as civilians were selling them on the black market, once they had taken them from dead soldiers. Some soldiers were even selling them on the black market, which meant guns were being passed around by different Firms now and kids and gangs as young as ten years old. They were simply getting hold of them just to impress other gangs or friends within them.

Even replica guns were being rebuilt by engineers now for a few hundred quid in some hidden workshop and they themselves were sold on the streets in most towns. Once used by who they were sold to they were then given back to different gangs that they had loaned them out from who had purchased them from the engineers in the first place. They had reconditioned the replicas to make them live fires again and were getting good money for doing so. Young and older were now shooting and stabbing each other on the streets side by side. These people knew they could make more money on these guns if they hired them out instead of getting rid of them once used.

The other Firms in London seemed to be doing well, until the Russian mafia moved in and started taking over bits of it. They were gaining more control of running things in the underworld and buying up different properties in and around London and pushing other well connected Firms out of the way.

Their money was now being used to invest in different projects, good and bad. The Russians were ruthless and didn't mess around. They made sure that it was 'do or die' with them and if they wanted it, they took it. They had no mercy with drug dealers who didn't pay their debts or anyone who tried to stand in their way. Anything they wanted they just took and asked questions later.

If it was already in illegal hands then it was more or less theirs, and no one could do much about it because they knew they were invisible. They had come over on fake passports or on the back of a lorry, so for them, it was survival. They could do what they had to do, and then be gone, out of the country again, on another false passport just like some of the yardies had done when they came and took parts of London over. They were militant.

The police wouldn't touch them if they were taking out the no good and other criminals. The more they got rid of, the less the police would have to worry about. The Russians would do the deeds and then be back on the boat or back in Moscow before the police had any leads on them. That's why there were more than 10,000 people still missing in London, allegedly and more illegal immigrants coming and going without a trace. That's why the Russians seemed invisible. Mess with the Russian Mafia and you would be erased, simple rules.

Everyone that lived to tell the tale knew it too. If you were smart you joined sides with them and became a force not to be reckoned with and you both would eliminate any Firm in London that tried to step into the arena. That's if you were smart enough and didn't get too greedy and try to out-smart them.

Mr Nice was smart and had worked with them too. He knew they would soon be running things over here because a Russian pole dancer he once dated told him all the things that were going on. She knew this all because her brother was very well connected in Moscow and Latvia. So, he had made it a point to build good relationships with them from the start, before they even came to London, which was a very shrewd move on his part. He had given two high Mafia figures somewhere to stay when they were on the run in Moscow for reasons Mr Nice never asked about and I can't talk about in this book, or ever if I to want to stay alive.

This had given Mr Nice some big brownie points for helping the two Russian fugitives. By doing this it had built good relationships between those Russians who were connected and those that were in the know. It meant Mr Nice could still run things but have the Russians backing him all the way in his business affairs, as he now had earned a trump card to call on with them for doing them the favour of looking after their men.

Mr Nice was also helping the fat cat Russian who was the link between him the Russian mafia. Mr Nice was asked to help him look for one of their good friends that had just disappeared without a trace. It turned out this missing Russian fella had some of their finance that he was looking after here in England but he had just vanished and had not contacted anyone they were connected to for months and it was of great importance for the fat cat Russian to find this man.

It only turned out to be the one that had the bank bonds that Old School had introduced me to when we were to do the deal out in South End with the drugs that Mr B got caught with. The one Johnny shot for shooting his mum. Mr Nice didn't know that, as the only ones that did know were me and Old School; we were there when it happened at Johnny's bar in Barbados.

Mr Nice told them he would help the Russian mafia find this fella. They were very grateful for his help. Within time and many meetings with this fat-cat Russian, Mr Nice still didn't have a clue where to look and he had nothing to go on with regards to finding this Russian for them, even though Mr Nice was pulling out all the stops. They were offering a large reward to whoever found him.

Mr Nice knew if he found him, he would be in good

stead with them and the Russian Mafia, he also knew he had to be the one to find him if his empire was ever going to get as big as it had become now. He then would be with them all the way, taking over parts of London. After so long with no leads. Mr Nice had asked Old School to help out to find this Russian with him.

So, at an underground fight in some old car park Mr Nice had come over to see a Russian fighter fight an American fella. Mr Nice told Old School that he needed to see him and wanted to talk with him, so at the fight Mr Nice told Old School that he needed his help as he took a pull of his cigar and then threw it on the floor.

"Mr Nice if I can help then let me know," said Old School.

The Russian had just made a mess of the American fighter that had been brought over for this organised underground fight.

"I need to find the Russian that was looking after some stolen bank bonds Old School. Keep your ears and eyes open son and tell me as soon as you hear or find him. Use my tab wherever you like in London. Just say put it on Mr Nice's tab okay? See, I look after you son don't I? Find him for me okay?"

Wong pulled up in the Bentley in the underground car park, everyone turned round to see just as Wong pressed the button on the Bentley to let down the tinted windows.

"Mr Nice you ready?" Wong asked. Mr Nice nodded.

"Hold on a minute"

He walked over to the Russian fighter who had just won the fight and shook his hand. Then Mr Nice walked over to the American fella who had organised the fight and he shook his hand too.

"Always a pleasure doing business with the Americans," Mr Nice said as he looked at the American organiser. He then passed him about seven grand. "Look, I'll be in touch when the next fight takes place."

"Okay Mr Nice," the American organiser said.

Mr Nice then pulled a grand out the bundle of fifties he had just been given by the American organizer and handed it back to him.

"Say hi to your boss in Miami for me."

"Will do Mr Nice."

Mr Nice inhaled on his cigar, took it out his mouth and trod it out. He shook the American's hand with the money tightly pushed inside his palm.

"Come on Old School."

Mr Nice walked over to Wong's Bentley and got in the back.

"Wong."

"Mr Nice."

"Here." He handed him a grand as well and placed the rest in his pocket. He had left Old School standing outside the blacked out window of the Bentley.

He slid down the window.

"Like I said Old School, find me that Russian fella and you can forget about what you owe me. You know the one that owned a gym? Somewhere in London."

He moved to roll the window up.

"Not the one Johnny killed is it?"

The window halted and then came down again.

"What?" Mr Nice said to Old school. "Say that again."

Old School was ushered into the Bentley and they drove to his gaff. Rifling through his drawers full of old records, drug related paraphernalia and not to mention a fair few shooters he picked up a crumpled photograph and showed it to Mr Nice.

"Look is that him?"

"It could be. Old School, it's time you met a good friend of mine."

Mr Nice said he wanted him to go with him to see some Russian Fat Cat who was eating in a posh restaurant in Mayfair London. Mr Nice and Old School walked into the restaurant. They were then shown to the table where the Fat-Cat Russian was eating.

"Sir, a guest of yours." the waiter said.

"Sit down," the Russian said. "Would you like something to eat or drink my friends?"

"No but I have this for you." Mr Nice handed him two grand from the money he had stashed in his pocket.

"I take it the fight went well and you're happy with our Russian fighter then?"

"I'm pleasantly impressed," smiled Mr Nice. "I had my doubts at first but he made a mess of the American fighter. Six weeks and they're getting a new one and they want to arrange another bet."

The Russian nodded.

"Okay then it's done."

"I will not be able to attend this one but I will be able to transfer the money to England the normal way to the exchange next to Wong's restaurant ready for Wong's minder to bring on the next fight for the betting. You know, the one the good looking Chinese girl? So, if you could attend the next one we can get Wong's minder to be there and place the bets with you."

"So be it," the Russian said.

Mr Nice said, "One more thing."

"Yes?"

"Old School show me that photo."

He passed it to Mr Nice who then showed it to the Fat Cat Russian.

As he chewed on the bit of steak he had just placed in his mouth, he put his knife and fork down slowly and then patted his mouth with the napkin. He then looked at the phone and showed it to the woman he was dining with. She looked and then spoke.

"That's him," she said in Russian. She had confirmed that the man they were looking for was him. It was the brother of the woman the Fat-Cat Russian was dining with.

"Where did you get this photo Mr Nice?"

Mr Nice Looked at Old School to get him to explain.

"Well?"

"He was someone I knew too," Old School said. "I did some work with him back in the day. He was well known in the strip clubs."

"That's him. That's our man Mr Nice," the Fat Cat said.

He looked at Old School with daggers in his eyes.

"Where did you last see him?"

"It was a few months ago."

"And?"

"Then there has been no more contact from him."

"So where do you think he could be now?"

"I'm not sure."

"Okay," Mr Nice said, "We will work on this for you. I'll be in touch."

"Make sure you do," the Fat Cat Russian said, "I have a lot riding on this Mr Nice."

"Yes, I'll be in touch."

Mr Nice then came out the restaurant with Old School.

They then got back into Wong's Bentley.

"Look Old School," said Mr Nice. "I don't think you understand how important this man is to me. To us. As you know Old School, I now need to find this man and I will not rest till we have him, do you hear me? Even if someone else finds him first then we will intercept them. So keep your ears and eyes open. I want this man Old School. If we can pull this off, then I will be running London and will not have to worry about any of them gangsters and Firms. I'll shit them. With this lot behind us, will be unstoppable Old School. We will have the whole place sewn up me old china. We need to find this man do you hear me Old School this is the key to London city."

That's when Old School said,

"Look Mr Nice, it was Johnny."

"What was?"

Wong placed the phone down and started up the Bentley. He pulled away from the restaurant in Mayfair and drove around London.

"Johnny killed this fella up in some shack near Johnny's bar out in Barbados. The one your Russian friends are looking for. I used to work with him ages ago Mr Nice. He owned a gay club called the Pink Pound in London. I was the DJ there and we clicked and started doing some work together with regards to drugs and clubs. He had a contact bring drugs over the water from Amsterdam. Then it all went pear-shaped as his missus owed on a batch of E's at their house and it had all gone downhill from there. One of the coppers had sort of said they knew what he was all about as they had him under surveillance, he had got really paranoid and had his team killed as he thought they were closing in on him and would soon grass him up."

Old School went on, "He had two of his Firm killed and had a copper bashed to fuck as he had found out that he was in our crew and came on his property in plain clothing or so he thought so he got his minder to shoot him. I was out in Cyprus D Jing. I had come back and heard the news from one of the Russian strippers he was seeing on the side. She said after this had happened, he had flown back to Moscow. He ended up losing the lot once the police were on his tail for the answers for his missus overdosing. Once the police were on to him, our little team fell apart and we all moved on once he had cut his ties with us. He then met up with some old friends but they had also got done for a massive fraud scam on credit card cloning. So, everyone involved went quiet and he laid low once everyone got nicked. But that was about seven years ago. I hadn't seen him for a bit. Then I rang him out he blue to get the Cookster out of trouble to see if he could pass some old contacts on to me and it was the Russian stripper that had answered he was still seeing her after all this time and we linked up again."

He continued, "It turned out he was ready to get back involved with the drugs himself and had a lot, and I mean a lot, of money and stolen bank bonds he had taken one out and given it to me for payment of the drugs. So we had sorted out a deal with some Colombians the Cookster and I had met with Mr B at Stringfellows. We were there and had seen them come in. They were a friend of a Cuban Firm that had great links to the cartel and had come over to Stringfellows to sort out some business arrangements. Mr B at the time was making the introduction for them both to work. It was the Colombians you paid off with a van load of money regards to the depot robbery money remember? Then my friend the Russian had got back on his feet and had bought a gym in Barnet, the Works, and was looking after some stolen bonds that had been smuggled over by one of their friends from St Petersburg. He said he was now working for a very rich and powerful Russian fella, which now I think must be the fella we have just met at the restaurant. Your mate the fat cat Russian. I then met up with him again and did the deal with him with one of the stolen bank bonds that he had given us out of the safe from the gym he was looking after for them. That helped the Cookster out of debt and we thought would have made me and the Cookster a lot of money ... Till it went pear shaped as you know. Well to cut a long story short Mr Nice, the fella in that photo; he got shot by Johnny as it turns out that this Russian here," he pointed to the photo again, "He had shot Johnny's Mum outside a casino in London for the Russian Mafia. The one your friend Theo owned when he was about twenty-two."

"What the fuck? Old School this is ain't good mate."

"Yes Mr Nice you'd better believe it."

"So, Johnny shot him? How do you know for sure this has happened?"

"Mr Nice ... it was me who had to bury him for Johnny. That's how I know mate. I was sitting there with the Cookster when Johnny had put one in his nut, out of the blue, as it was this Russian who had sorted out their passport with Murph to get them out there. When we had got them out of the prison van."

"Fuck me ... So Cookster knows about this too does he?"

"Yes Mr Nice."

"So, it was Johnny that killed him?"

"Yes Mr Nice, that's what I just said."

"Now we are fucked."

Mr Nice passed this info onto the Russian Fat Cat, and was now also connected but he did not talk about Old School's part in it all or about me being present when the killing had taken place.

Mr Nice had taken the Fat Cat Russian with Old School and some of the Russian Fat Cat's friends to Barbados to the grave where their dead Russian man lay. One of the fellas that had come with the Russian Fat Cat was an Italian mafia crime boss, and also in this motley crew was the woman Old School met with the Fat Cat Russian while having dinner in Mayfair, when Mr Nice had taken him along to meet him after the underground fight.

When they got to the grave, they gave Old School a shovel and told him to dig.

For that split instance he had thought Mr Nice had told them that it was him that had buried him and that they would get rid of him for Mr Nice as he now knew what Mr Nice had done with the stolen depot money with the deal made with the Colombians.

"Dig him up," the Russian Fat Cat said.

Old school did as he was told.

The Fat Cat Russian became very rich because he was the one who organised for the bonds to go missing from an insider, his brother, a Russian agent working in England for the MI5. He had connections within the houses of parliament and had discovered that the treasury would be moving bonds from the vaults signed and ready for the release of the gold ready for the royal mint to start printing more bank notes. The agent had given inside information about what was happening and that they were to be transported. So they had a courier bodyguard come and pick them up by motorbike and he left with the bank bonds at 1:30 in the morning.

The Russian agent had passed this all on to his brother. While the courier was driving the bike, a car pulled out in front of him and a van pulled up alongside and the driver of the bike hit the car and was thrown clear. He flew straight over the car and landed heavily in the road. He just lay there as he was shot and then thrown into the river Thames together with his bike.

The parcel was then picked up and a call was made.

"We have your parcel sir."

The Fat Cat Russian was sitting on a bench outside the hotel, waiting for the bonds to come. All of a sudden a motorbike pulled up at the lights in Marble Arch and the biker let the parcel free. It landed on the floor and he drove off at speed. The Russian then walked out and picked up the parcel and walked it to the Grosvenor hotel and then opened the parcel to reveal the bonds and passports.

He called room service and ordered a bottle of champagne and the person who had ordered the transfer of the bonds stepped down and left the houses of parliament and met the now Fat Cat Russian at the hotel. They split some of the bonds with the Russian agent who had then gone on to a restaurant and had had a meal, but was poisoned as government officials received some of the bonds back. They picked up the case and then left, poisoning him. The government official that had worked with the Russian agent and had grassed him up, unbeknownst to the government officials. That's why they had him killed, stepped down and retired. He had had some of the bonds cashed and had settled down out in Dubai without anyone knowing that he had set up the Russian agent that was the now fat cat's brother by turning him in to the government officials.

The Fat Cat Russian had the rest and had got the Russian woman's brother that Mr Nice and Old School had met at the restaurant in Mayfair to look after the stolen bonds for him in a safe house, which turned out to be the gym. The government officials had been all over him for years trying to see if the stolen bonds would show up but they had stopped as they were spending too much of the tax payers' money on him and finding nothing. He was doing everything very shrewdly and had sneaked a few of the bonds out to South Africa in return for the Kruger hands.

The government tried to cancel the bonds but some had already been used. The bonds that had been cancelled were worth nothing.

No one else knew this as it was kept quiet, but the government had put on red alert to all the banks that if they turned up then the authorities should be told straight away so they could come and arrest anyone that used them. But to the crime world and anyone else on the black market, they were as good as money and were still being passed around by the Russian Fat Cat now all the heat had died.

So, they were paying others in their Firm to smuggle diamonds and Kruger hands over to this gym from South Africa with these bonds with using some of them. The rest were all stashed in the gym in Barnet for safe keeping. Then it came to light that they were indeed aware that the bonds had now been cancelled, as a drug lord had been nicked trying to cash one in Romania for an arsenal of guns.

The only one who knew it was there were me and Old School and the dead Russian that Johnny had killed. Come to think of it we should have gone there and got it all for ourselves, but we missed that as we had the Colombians after us for the cocaine that was stopped in Southend, and we were too busy with the depot robbery.

Old School dug a little more and the body was uncovered. Old School pulled the decomposing body out of the ground a little more as they watched.

"That's enough," the Fat Cat Russian said as Old School pulled. They could still see the tattoo on the dead Russian's decaying arm. They turned to the Russian women who confirmed it was the missing Russian.

They were grateful to Mr Nice for finding out the information on him and for bringing him to confirm it was their man. That's when the Sicilian mafia man, who had also come over to see for himself, wanted to shoot Old School, as he thought that the only person that would know where the dead Russian was must have been his killer. He got out of the car with his loaded gun and pointed it at Old School, who was standing in the grave.

The Russian woman nodded at the Italian Mafia man.

"Stop!" Mr Nice told him it was Johnny who did the killing.. The Fat Cat Russian then stopped the Italian Mafia man and made him put the gun away. He was gutted that he was dead and also gutted that Johnny was already dead and it wasn't them that had killed him, as they would have fed him to the lions.

"Old School was just doing what he was being told to do so, as I said, put the gun down."

"Yes," Old School said "That's right. Now put the gun away you're making me nervous. It's normally me holding the shooter, not me looking down the barrel of gun." He tried to joke.

"Okay," the Italian Mafia man said.

"Fill in the grave and let's get out of here. This is giving me the creeps," said Mr Nice.

Mr Nice and the main Fat Cat Russian boss had become good friends after this. Old School had pulled it off again. Mr Nice had gotten on so well with the Fat Cat Russian after this that when the Russian Fat Cat offered Mr Nice the ten grand reward for finding the missing Russian, Mr Nice refused.

"Look, I don't want the money." The Russian was surprised.

"I want to work with you," said Mr Nice, "Keep the money."

He knew that to make a contact like this with the Fat Cat Russian and the Italian Mafia and work with them was priceless. Worth much more than a little ten grand and a 'thanks very much' handshake.

After that, they had gone on to do business with each other for his help in helping them put things to rest and for finding the gym with all the stuff still safely stuck in a safe under the floor. Old School had also taken them to the gym that the dead Russian owned and had taken us to back then when we had got the stolen bank bond for the meeting with Mr B to pay for the cocaine that came in to Southend.

When Mr B and one of the divers had been nicked, the other diver had escaped with two keys of Colombia's finest cocaine. The rest of them had been arrested and were still serving time right now.

Now the main Fat Cat Russian could finally get the rest of the bank bonds that were all still stashed in there for safe keeping inside the gym. He planned to take them back to Moscow and the hands that had been smuggled over here would stay, as every one of them was an ounce of pure gold, and he knew that gold would soon be rising in price.

The Fat Cat Russian was using the gym as a safe house whilst out here in England. Mr Nice had asked what all this was for and the Fat Cat Russian said it will be for the time when we can get a load of passports or some arms.

The Russians were very loyal to Mr Nice, now he was connected to the Russian and were helping each other with his business matters.

CHAPTER 21

I remembered when Don F was ready for Johnny when he came out of the nick, to get the money that was buried by the Asian off licence owner. They had found out it was buried in the timeshare. Johnny was the only other person who knew where the money was buried. The other half belonged to Don F once they met in Marbella to dig it up. Johnny would give a bit of his money to Mr Nice for a share in the cocaine field, so would the Sicilian mob man.

They didn't know at the time that it had all been destroyed and that Johnny was the one who had shot the two Asian brothers for Don F.

We didn't know that they had, and would, make money from it as Old School and I were doing a favour for Mia and Old School in the hope that, once it was done and all sorted, he would get into Jenny's pants. . And guess what? One night when they were both buzzing on E's in a pirate radio station, as he was spinning the decks, yes, they had sex.

The Bradford mob wanted to get more drugs to make more money to buy the cash and carry but Mia's dad didn't want to sell. He said,

"If you get this amount, then I might think about it." He only said this to stop them causing trouble for him and Mia. He didn't really want to sell, even though they were threatening him and his daughter, continuously and giving him grief, smashing up his car and his daughter's flat to bits before she moved out from one of their Firm members. Even though they kept coming round saying they would give him this amount, he said *no* every time. They would cause problems, and smash his windows and his car so he would tell them to come back once they had x amount and he'd think about it. This was just a lie to keep them sweet for now and stop them causing him and his daughter problems and to stop them from harassing her.

The Asian Bradford mob thought if they spent half the money that they got from the stolen drugs their dad had bought from the dead farmer, then they could turn it around in no time and have enough money to buy the cash and carry right out, this time with an offer he couldn't refuse, and a little more for themselves.

The last time they came to see the cash and carry owner's daughter, she misinformed them. She told the gang member, who she was once seeing, that she didn't want to get back with him but she could help them get some cheap drugs to pay off the Bradford Firm. She said they were cheap, enough to meet the price her dad asked for, but the deal was, they had to leave them alone. They agreed. This was all part of the plan. She said that the only people that had, or could sort out drugs in this quantity, would be the South Americans or a Sicilian Firm that her friend knew.

Before long, they were directed to a close contact of the Sicilian Mafia boss. This Mafia boss had hired Johnny as hired hands for this job. After I talked with Mia, she told her ex that she knew a man that could help them get their drugs as long as they left her family alone. It would be enough to pay of the heroin debt at least and enough for him to leave the gang. After the ex-spoke to the Asian gang members about it, they said they would agree, if he could sort it out, but they were lying.

They just wanted the money for the cash and carry. She told them about a very good friend of Don F's, in fact, it was his nephew, who owned a barbers shop in Regent Street in London. She told them to go to the barbers and see a man called Lorenzo and he would help them.

They walked in to the barbers and took a seat.

"Yes fellas what can I do …?"

"We're not here for a haircut. We're here to talk to Lorenzo."

They were told to wait. Once the last customer had had his hair cut, the man walked to the front door and then turned the sign around so it read 'closed' before addressing the brothers.

"Okay fellas, what can I do for you?

"We're here to see Lorenzo."

"You're talking to him my friend."

Then the deal was organised. They didn't have a clue they had all been set up very well and that they would soon be talking to Don F on the phone. They were not organising the big drug deal they thought they were scoring, but they were organising their funerals. One of the Asian brothers had told the mob boss that the arrangement would be half the money up front and the other would be kept safe buried in a garden in Spain in a timeshare. They wanted to know if they would still do the deal if they gave them the key to the timeshare, as their dad had taken it over there for a rainy day. He would pass the key to him once the deal was done between them.

The brothers now had the key and wanted to make sure they weren't being set up feeling a little unsure about doing this deal. Once the deal had been done, they would then hand the door key over to Don F. It was just a precaution for them and they felt safe doing business like this as they continued to talk to him on the phone.

"Okay," Don F said. "It's not how I normally do business but, however you want to play, it is fine by me as business is business. As long as I get paid like you say I will, then you have a deal and if I don't, then I will find you and you will leave this world faster than you came into it. Do you understand me? I don't normally do things like this. Business is normally done on my terms and my terms only, but I can see this is a big step for you and I'm willing to work this way this time around until a little trust has been built between us. Can I ask you just in case you could be Old Bill, where did the money come from?"

"What? Who gives a fuck where it came from?" demanded the first brother. "Look, it was given to us on a loan by our Dad."

"Nice Dad," the mob boss said.

"Yes, it was compensation, an insurance pay-out as the old man owned an off licence but it had been torched by some racists."

Don F was well aware of this but hid the fact he knew it wasn't done in a racial attack, but he went along with it. They didn't know, but it was in fact Malcolm's men that had done it for a giving the old man a warning by Mr Nice to try to get the drop of cocaine back.

That's when Don F knew for sure that they had got the

money from the stolen cocaine and maybe a few quid from their own antics and things they were involved with also like Viagra, jelly ones, steroids and heroin. They also were involved in a big cut and shut scam and stealing cars and shipping them abroad as they had divulged voluntarily all this to the Sicilian mob man.

So, he figured he would get the money back they had stolen. They were falling for it all the way to the bank. Greed plays a big part in every fuck up, and most men and women fail because of greed. Half the money had indeed been brought to the arranged meeting in the underground car park, the same car park where the Russian and the American had their in fight two weeks ago; the fight Mr Nice had attended. The other bit of money was in the garden at the timeshare in Spain as they said on the phone to the Sicilian mob man. It was all set to meet the Bradford mob brothers there.

The Asian Firm thought they were being smart by doing this with the money; having half buried and half on delivery. They thought their money would be safe by doing business like this. This was a new contact and they were just being careful. Can't blame them can you? So, they had come to the meeting arranged by Don F thinking that they would soon walk away with more drugs than they had money for. That was the promise.

"Just give me the key to the timeshare on the meet and we will have a deal, okay?"

"Yes." The phone went dead.

The brothers knew that they would now have enough money to buy the cash and carry and they were very excited. This was an offer the Bradford brothers' Firm couldn't refuse. Once they had the drugs from this deal sold and with a little heavy persuasion on the owner from them, the cash and carry was theirs.

They were willing to pay well over the odds for it even though Mia's dad had set a price on it just to get rid of them the last time they had turned up and caused havoc. Once they had this lot sorted, the cash and carry would be theirs and the heroin debt would be paid for. Or so they thought.

Now Don F had found out about this money in Spain, he wanted Johnny to come to the meeting in the car park with him to take care of business before he had took care of me. Then once he had he wanted, Johnny was to go to Spain with him to collect the rest of the money so they could share it out. Then Johnny would be able to send it over to Mr Nice in the hope he would give Johnny, and in turn Don F, a share in his Colombian field. But now Johnny had got himself killed.

He was no longer going to be around to meet the Sicilian Mafia boss to dig up the money. Don F was the only person who knew the location of the time share, but he had got himself nicked as well. Therefore, he was blissful about what had happened to Johnny but after trying to phone Mandy to contact him from prison, he finally thought that the only other person he could and would trust to get it, would be Mr Nice. But if the prison guards knew something wasn't right they would notify the police for sure.

The mob boss's wife would be watched by the police's intelligent services now too, since he had been banged up. They would be keeping a track on his and her bank accounts now that money was going in and out. He had to be smart and think about his every move. He told her to leave Manchester and to go and stay out in Spain.

Things hadn't gone quite as Johnny and the Sicilian

mob boss had planned after the deal was done with the Asian brothers in the underground car park. Johnny went to Mandy's funeral and then on to the time share to meet the Sicilian mob to get the buried money. But as you know Johnny met his creator during the process!

The Sicilian boss's wife had found out that he had been nicked, she went to see him in prison on a visit. She knew the police had raided her house in Manchester. On the prison visits they would talk to each other in code, but to everyone else listening in it was a normal chat, and they made sure that it could be heard so it looked like a normal visit was taking place. They didn't want to arouse any suspicion amongst the guards or the police.

The police and guards didn't have a clue what was going on, even though the police had planted bugs below the tables he was sat at during all his visits. The police had their ideas about him now that he was in custody and they knew that he would talk to them eventually but only on his terms, and not at the risk of others in his family.

He didn't want them getting in trouble because he witnessed things that was very interesting to the police and he knew he had to somehow get the money back that he had hidden in a Marbella bank, but he didn't know how he was going to do it just yet. Once he was on witness protection, they would know that the money was immoral and he would lose the lot, and he didn't want that.

No members of the criminal organisation came to see him or his family, and they were told not to even attempt to. If they did, the police would take their fingerprints and photos and they would know who was who, and who he was connected to. They were all told not to even write letters to him. No contact whatsoever.

He knew the police had more on him that they were letting on, and he knew they were just biding their time with him. It could swing both ways; if they nicked him for something more serious, he wouldn't be able to stand in court and give the evidence they needed to put the other Firm member away, as this member, had shot a judge outside the court.

But, he wanted to try to get away from them if he could. He knew a good plastic surgeon to conceal his identity. If he needed to, he could give them the slip as he stood a better chance getting a new fresh unnoticed income from Mr Nice's field once he or Johnny had the money from the timeshare. While he was sitting there on association watching the news in prison he had heard that the English money was changing.

The news had come out that everyone should take their old ten, twenty and fifty pound notes into the banks as they were going out of circulation, and change them for the new ones.

If anyone missed the cut off day that had been set by the bank of England and the government, then they would lose their money, as it would no longer be welcomed as tender and would not be worth anything.

As you can imagine, there was a big rush and panic for everyone to exchange their money for these new notes before the dead line and they were no longer in circulation. The old money would have no value and wouldn't be accepted anywhere any more. It would be just as good as Monopoly money; worthless. Don F watched in disbelief at first as he thought it was a big wind up but as he watched and listened carefully to the TV reporter, he then realised it wasn't a wind up after all and that it was very true and serious.

He sat in his seat a bit more, really panicking and concerned about what the TV reporter was now saying. He listened intensely and it had registered what was being said.

"Hang on a minute …" the Sicilian mob boss said to the other inmate who wanted to turn the TV over. "…I want to hear this."

"Come on, who wants to listen to this stuck in here?"

"I do, so just wait. I need to see this my friend, leave it there."

He went mad when he had heard the news. *Shit £250,000 down the pan! Mama Mia.* He knew the buried money was all in English notes.

This was the money he was depending on and that had been buried, ready for Johnny to collect, but there had been no show from Johnny so he assumed it was still buried safe and sound and he knew it was as Johnny was now dead!

If he didn't act fast, then the money would be no good to anyone. The money had come from a deal the Sicilian boss set up in England with the Asian brothers. They wanted a shipment of brown to come over and he said he was the man to sort it out for them as had been set up by us. He had hired Johnny to come to the meeting with the two Bradford brothers. There was never going to be any real drug deal. This meeting was just so the Sicilian boss could have the money back that they had nicked in the first place from Mr Nice, for the parcel the pilot had dropped into the wrong field.

So, the meeting was set up as the Asian men arrived for the heroin. They shook hands as the Sicilian mob man then walked them to the mob boss's car leaving their other friend in their BMW.

"Okay, you are going to like what I have for you." They

were very excited as he asked where the money was. They had got out of the car empty handed.

"My brother is there with the key for the timeshare as we said."

"So, where's my money?"

"It's in the car with our friend. Once I see the goods, then we will give you the money, okay?"

"Okay. Where is the timeshare?"

"Look I have everything you need. It's in Spain." He gave the address. "So just show me the goods and then we can do the deal and move on from all this."

They walked round to the boot of the Sicilian boss's car.

"This is top gear and you will not be disappointed."

The mob boss then popped open the boot. As it raised up, the other fella they had sitting waiting for them in the car lost sight of them.

He then heard two little spit pops. Johnny had shot them both just as the boot opened. He then got out of the boot and helped the Sicilian mob boss push them into the boot and then closed it down. They then both walked over to the other car where the other Asian brother was sitting. None the wiser of what had happened until Johnny raised the gun up and the boot had been shut. He tapped it on the window of their car.

"Open up."

"Shit." The Asian guy started the car up.

Johnny smashed the window, grabbed the keys and banged him in the head with the gun. The mob boss then walked forward to get into the Asian man's car. One of the other Asians that Johnny had shot climbed out of the boot with the mob's shotgun and raised it up.

"Stay there."

"Is everything okay fellas?"

The Asian man shouted to Johnny to put the gun down. Johnny moved to put it down and he let off a shot, hitting the Asian fella in the nuts. It was a tense moment as the Asian fella fell to his knees, blazing the shotgun into the wall behind the Sicilian mob boss. Johnny then walked over, kicked him to the floor, picked up the shotgun and put it in the Asian man's car. He then walked over to their driver.

"Okay, where's the money?" the Sicilian mob boss asked the other Asian, who was sitting in the car holding his head. "Also, the key for the timeshare."

"I don't know."

"Well, if you can't tell me where my money is, then Johnny here will give you a hand finding it."

"Do what you like, I ain't telling you nothing. Look I don't know where it is. Do your worst."

"Out of the fucking car now," Johnny yelled dragging him out himself, he head-butted him and then started hitting him, almost knocking him out.

"Do what you like. I'm not telling you anything," the Asian fella repeated as he fell to the floor.

Johnny walked over to their car, got into it and started it up. He reversed it back with a skid, and then slammed his foot on the accelerator with a wheel spin rushing forward in the path of the Asian. The Asian turned over to see what was going on and as he tried to stand up, he saw the car coming towards him at speed and cried out in fear.

"Okay, I'll tell you! Stop!"

The mob boss heard him and shouted for Johnny to stop and waved his hands. Johnny skidded the car to a halt, about three inches from the trembling Asian man. The Asian man stumbled as he tried to stand up.

"Okay, okay. The money's in the boot under the spare wheel."

The Sicilian boss had a look and, sure enough the money was there, just as he said, all nicely wrapped up in crisp notes from the bank.

"Okay. Where's the key for the timeshare?"

Johnny put the dead Asian brother in the boot of their car and then slammed the boot shut again. He pulled out a knuckle duster and banged the Asian on the side of the head.

"Goodnight," he said to the man he had just roughed up, knocking him out.

The Sicilian boss then put his hand into his pocket and pulled out the key out for the timeshare.

Johnny bundled the knocked out Asian into the boot of the car with his dead friends. He then placed the gun he had used to shoot the two brothers into the knocked out Asian's hands. Johnny then placed an eighth of cocaine in the knocked out Asian's pocket before picking up the Asian man's mobile. He walked calmly over to the Sicilian boss, who was now waiting in the car. They drove slowly, out of the underground car park and Johnny made a call to the police using the Asian man's phone.

"Quickly! I have heard gunshots in an old disused underground car park. Come quickly I have just seen a blue BT van come skidding out," he lied.

"Okay sir, stay on the line," the emergency services said, but Johnny had already pushed the button on the phone and disconnected them.

They drove on with the key and the address to the timeshare and some of the stolen money from the deal that they had nicked from the farmer, which belonged to Mr Nice. The Sicilian boss drove Johnny to the subway.

"Pull in here." Johnny got out and leaned back in through the window.

"Okay, so where's my money?"

The Sicilian boss laughed.

"Look my friend, you just heard the man. Our money is in the garden of the villa. This lot is coming with me." He pointed to the bag. "This is to sort out with Mr Nice about the cocaine field so me and you can get a share in it. Once he hears I have this money he will say yes as he has just lost this lot and to get it back not knowing it's his. He will give us a share, you'll see. Leave it to me. Here …," The Sicilian boss threw him a bundle of notes. "That will keep you going for now. Our bit is in the villa. Once we get to the villa I'll sort Mr Nice out with regards to the field okay?"

Johnny nodded.

"You know I will find you and you know I will get back what is mine."

"Johnny, you have my word."

"You have my word too. I will put a bullet in the back of your nut while you sleep if you try to fuck me."

"Your money will come back to you tenfold once we get to the villa and I get Mr Nice to split a percentage of the field with us using his own money. Look, we can go there in a few days and dig the rest up then you'll be there when I talk to Mr Nice about the field. It will give you time to sort out your other business first with your sister."

He threw the Asian man's phone off the bridge they had driven over and it had been crushed by oncoming cars. Johnny then looked back at the Sicilian boss as they drove on.

Then Johnny agreed.

"Okay. See you in Spain in three days."

He had to sort out something quick which was to attend his sisters funeral then go out to Spain to meet up with the Sicilian mob to get the time share money. "I will meet you there in five days then."

"Okay." Johnny pulled the key out of his pocket. "Just some reassurance." He had pick-pocketed the Sicilian boss for the key as they drove along.

He walked through the subway and got into his sports Land Rover car and then drove to Wong's restaurant in China Town.

Johnny had gotten killed before he had a chance to meet with Don F boss over in Spain at the villa ready to dig the money up.

After the deal they had done in Manchester, Don F had gone back home to Sicily after the meeting with the Asian brothers to lay low for a bit. Then on the third day, had gone out to Spain to meet Johnny at the villa, to dig up this money and to do the deal with Mr Nice with regards to the field. Mr Nice didn't know any of this just yet.

Don F knew Johnny had the key so he waited knowing once he was there they could just go in and dig up the money but he too was arrested outside the villa. As he arrived, he sat there for a bit and waited, he decided to phone Mandy to get in touch with Johnny but there was no answer, so he waited but no show, so he thought, *Fuck it.*

He walked over to the garden, kicked the back gate off, and was ready to walk into the garden and dig it up himself. He thought that Johnny may have already dug it up and that's why he didn't show up. The neighbour next door sunbathing by the pool had phoned the police. They pulled up and he saw them out of the corner of his eye and walked back out of the garden then he looked at his watch and was hoping Johnny would turn up with the key and they then could make up a story as to why he had kicked the gate open. He looked down at his watch then looked up trying to look calm, but the police officer came over to him and asked him what he was doing.

"Hi sir."

Then both police come over to him but as he tried to shy away from them, subtly walking over towards his car, they stopped.

"Yes officers, how can I help you?"

"What's your name sir? You seem to be causing some damage sir."

"I'm just waiting for a friend. He told me to kick the back gate open because he lost the key or he is looking for it. He will be here soon."

"Okay, sir come and sit in our car and we'll see if he turns up."

Johnny didn't turn up.

When they had asked for his name gave them a false one, but to his surprise, it had come back as *wanted*. Then, he gave them his real name and the control said he was wanted on tax evasion charges, which was a bit strange. He was wanted for a charge for tax evasion and that he was a key witness in a case of murder of a judge out in Sicily and the police had been trying to summon him but he was no longer at the address he had given them at the time. So, they had arrested him on a tax evasion charges before he had a chance to get to the money he was so close to.

He had received five months on remand and then he was let go. The court dismissed the charge as the police wanted him for this trial and wanted to keep him a clean witness.

While he was inside serving time, he had tried to

contact Johnny as he only trusted Johnny now with what was going on, and he had also tried to phone Mandy, Johnny's sister, several times from the nick to get hold of him. He wanted to see if he had turned up after all and to see if he had got the money for them and to explain what had happened to him and why he wasn't there to meet him, but it was to no joy. If he could contact Mandy or Johnny then they could meet up once he got out. If they hadn't got the money then they could get the money and he could pay Johnny what he owed him for doing his dirty work for him and then sort out with Mr Nice for the field.

There was still no answer from either of them every time he tried calling. He knew the police would be listening to him on the phone and bugging his visits so he had to take care of what he was doing.

Unbeknown to him, Mandy had also been shot and killed at the Savoy Hotel in London by the hit men for the money I owed the Columbians for the deal that had gone terribly wrong in Southend with regards to the drug deal sorted out in Stringfellows that night. The one Mr B and one of the drivers had gone down for as the other one had got away with the two keys of cocaine.

I had been given one back when we had met, which was a weird thing as I have never seen him again and nor has anyone else in the criminal system who we were involved with. The Sicilian boss would phone Mandy when he wanted to get a message through to Johnny normally, but there was now no answer from either of them, so he was panicking a little. He had taken a risk to try to phone him directly. He went mad inside and smashed the phone and kicked the bin. Then went to his cell.

The next day, he sat down to watch TV and saw the

news flash about the English money.

"No, no, no!" He had jumped up and grabbed a phone card from one of the inmates and barged another off the phone so he could use it.

"Chill out man," the fellow inmate said to the Sicilian boss.

"Look, keep talking and you'll be chilling out for the rest of your days. I'll put you in the morgue." The Sicilian boss squared up to him. "Look, man I need the phone."

He grabbed his balls and told him to do one. Then he quickly punched in the number. The fella was standing there with water in his eyes and the Sicilian mob man yelled at him again.

"Fuck off! You're like a bad smell still hanging around. So do one."

He had got through to his wife in Manchester. He told her to get in touch with Mandy's dad. He was bluffing.

"His name is Mr Nice. I need some gardening done in our villa; number 35 San Tonyia, in Spain okay?" He gave the address. "I have lost the key but the gate is open," He lied. He knew the key was with Johnny. "So, look you might have to just get in the garden. The back gate is open. I need the garden taken care of dig and plant new flowers in the garden for me. Go with him to the villa and help him in to the garden in Spain. Then get Mr Nice, Mandy's father to help you out over there and then come over to Marbella to meet me so I can chat to him once I get my release."

"What?" she asked.

"Just do it. Do as you are told woman. I tell you, do you hear me?"

He had just given her the number for Mandy's Dad but it was a bluff and was really Mr Nice's.

"Ask her Dad to help you. Get him to help you dig the

garden over. I know your back is bad and the roses are probably overgrown by now, me being stuck in here doesn't help."

The prison guards then told the inmates to bang up again and said hurry up otherwise he would shut off the phone as he walked past the Sicilian boss. He then walked off and started locking prisoners behind their doors. Then as the screw walked back again, he saw the Sicilian man still on the phone.

"Bang up now or …"

"Look I need to …"

"Bang up now or go to the block."

The guard looked at the other guard, who then turned off the power to the phone anyway. The phone went dead.

"Fuck!" the Sicilian man shouted as he hung up the phone.

His wife hung up too. She now had a phone number given to her and was told to phone.

She called the number.

"Hi, is that Mandy's dad?"

"No, sorry darling you have the wrong number."

"Is this Mr Nice?"

"Who's this darling? How did you get this number?"

"The Cosanostra gave it to me. The Sicilian mob boss."

"Okay, I need you to come over to Spain to meet me."

"I'm the Sicilian boss's wife."

"Yes I know now, say no more."

"I live in Spain darling so I'll meet you here."

"I have been told to show you a villa by my husband out there."

"Sorry?"

"We need to meet up."

"Okay. I will come and meet you. Come to Spain."

So, Mr Nice was a bit unsure with what she had said.

He had arranged to bump into Don F's wife conveniently so as to not draw too much attention to themselves. She feared the police were watching her every move now as they also raided their house in Manchester when he had got nicked.

So she went over to Spain from Manchester specifically for this meeting and to pass on the message to Mr Nice that she had received from her husband. She met Mr Nice and had explained what the Sicilian Mafia boss wanted him to do.

"Gardening." She explained.

"What? I'm not the sort of fella to do that darling."

She said that Don F had told her to tell you to take good care of the rose bushes in his villa.

"I never knew he had but then again there's a lot I don't know. I only get to know the half of what he has and hasn't got and what he's involved in."

"It's probably best you don't." Mr Nice said.

"He said, you need to dig the Garden over."

She said he would soon be out and would want Mr Nice to sail to Marbella to meet him in person once he had gotten out of prison, once he had dug the garden over. She said that she had arranged for the Sicilian mobs' yacht, with all the crew, to sail him over there to meet the Sicilian boss on the pier. The Sicilian boss's wife had confirmed a meeting would take place in Marbella between him and her husband once he had done this favour.

The next day, Mr Nice and Wong, went to the villa. Wong had come out to see Mr Nice as there seemed to be some problems he was having back in London. They dug up the garden with the Sicilian boss's wife but they found nothing there. Had Johnny already got to it? Or were the Bradford Firm, the Asian brothers, lying?

Mr Nice walked over to the other roses that were in a

pot and pulled the plant pot that had one white rose in it. He lifted up the slab and dug into the loose soil. Nothing.

He then turned and saw a casting of an elephant. He moved it. The shovel went ding as it touched a box just below the soil, so he dug round it and pulled it up.

They opened the box and there it was just as the dead Asian brother had said it was back in Manchester before Johnny had finished him off. There was £250,000 in different note denominations, neatly stashed in bundles in the box that were soon to be useless unless you were a collector of old bank notes.

Now they had the money, they had to move fast. Mr Nice thought it would be a good idea if they changed it all up into Euros so there wouldn't be as much in notes and it would be easier to carry.

They slung the box onto the wheelbarrow and covered it with brambles and soil and then covered it with dirt and put it on the van with the other rubbish.

Mr Nice and Wong and Don F's wife then drove from the villa to the garage at the house she was renting while staying in Spain. They then got the box out and pulled it open again and looked at the money. It was all bundled up in a clear blue bag.

"Well thanks fellas," the wife said "I'll take it all from here."

Mr Nice laughed.

"Look, he told us to get it and meet him with it, did he not? Not leave it with you."

"What you trying to say?"

"Look, let's just get it changed up. No disrespect, but I would like to meet him with it. Then I know I have done what he has asked and there can be no mistakes and I know

I have given it to him personally. You understand."

"Yes."

"Then there can be no mistakes or confusion from your husband."

She then shut the money box.

"Well, I think we need to change it like you said, before the currency changes."

"What?"

"Didn't you see the news?"

"Fuck," said Mr Nice, "Let's get busy and get this lot changed into Euros."

He put some of the money through one of Johnny's mate's car businesses to clean up quickly. Some of it went to a fella that owned a Limousine business and was banked and changed into the new notes and then drawn on a transfer in Euros. Mr Nice and Wong changed the lot into Euros at different places and post offices and travel agents, hotels and his own restaurant and through the exchange next door.

They had now got the money sorted all into Euros they had also bought a load of traveller's cheques and cashed them, this made it a lot easier to handle. Her husband was stuck in the nick and didn't know what was going on and had hoped that the message had got through to Mr Nice and that the money would be in safe hands by now ready for him to collect if it was still in fact there and Johnny hadn't got to it already.

Looking out of the prison window, he watched the birds play and thought to himself for a moment; if he didn't move fast on his release then the police would have him and his money, well, only the money they knew about. Anything else he could make he could stash up to get at a later stage once everything had calmed down in regards to the police and the plans and enquiries to the family feud that was going on and with regards to one of the Sicilian court judges being murdered in a big high profile case that he had witnessed.

The newly laundered money was then placed in two small luggage cases in evenly shared amounts, give or take a few Euros, ready for Don F's release. He would be ready to leave prison in Marbella very soon. Mr Nice and Wong had the money all safe and sound in their midst. So, now the time had come for Don F to be released from prison and the Mafia boss's wife to organise for Mr Nice to get on their yacht and sail to Marbella ready for their meeting.

The Sicilian boss was a bit apprehensive as to whether the money had been secured for the meeting or not, but he would still attend in the hope that his wife had done as she was told. He was short and sweet on the phone but he had been interrupted before he had a chance to finish off the conversation in prison to confirm to his wife what had been said the next day.

The day of Don F's release was a balmy luscious summer's afternoon and as he waited outside the prison with the sun beaming down, a black MX5 pulled up. It was driven by a Russian who was a bodyguard.

"Private boss," the Russian said.

The bodyguard looked a bit like Dolph Lunglund out of the Rocky films; a very tall big muscular guy with his spiky hair. Don F got into the Jeep.

"Here I have your shirt ready for you as you asked."

"Pull over here so I can change."

The bodyguard passed the shirt from the back to the Mafia boss, who then changed before he sat in the front seat.

"Okay. Where to?"

"Drive down to the harbour. We have some business to take care of before I go meet any family members. We are going to meet an old acquaintance of mine, I hope. I haven't seen him now for nearly ten years. We worked together for five of those ten years without even seeing each other's faces."

"Okay."

The Russian drove on. Unbeknownst to them, a white van had also pulled onto the same road and was staying far back behind them. It had followed them from the prison.

As the Jeep moved on forward towards the harbour the van continued to follow.

CHAPTER 22

Mr Nice was sailing across the water on the mob boss's yacht that had been told to pick him up by the Sicilian mobs boss's wife. He said goodbye to her and she said good luck. Mr Nice gave her a lump of money from his jacket pocket.

"I'm sure if he wants you to have more he will organise the rest to come over to you once I hand this over to him."

She thanked him as he and Wong got out of the rented Maserati then they boarded the mobs yacht. It was nearly time for Mr Nice to meet the Sicilian boss again.

He could now also let Don F know the bad news about Johnny and Mandy's death. He didn't want to talk on the phone. They didn't like to talk about business over the phone as they knew they could easily be traced and monitored by the police GPS.

The police could track your every move and pinpoint where you were and also record what you were saying on any call. It was common knowledge that the mob was being bugged and that everything should be and was said by word of mouth once you had been searched for listening devices. Now the Sicilian boss's son had been killed; mowed down outside the court with the judge, it had confirmed that it was all best to talk face to face nowadays as the police wouldn't rest until all those that were involved in the drugs Triad had been caught and were rotting behind bars.

Things were being written down on a note in a code language only we could understand and once the correct receiver had got it, he would then set fire to it to destroy the evidence to avoid it falling into the wrong hands and before the police were able to work out what was going on or what was written. They even used ultra violet lights sometimes so if they got raided on first impressions the paperwork seemed to be blank. But once the ultra violet light was used, the police would then see all the documentation and the things that were going to be done or had been. Doing things this way meant no one had to even speak to each other if we felt or knew somewhere had been bugged.

Things were getting too close for comfort. The police had now found the Don, the boss of the mob family, the one the Sicilian mob boss had witnessed doing the murder. They had caught him after twelve long years of hiding. He had been caught by a tip off as his clean clothes had arrived at his hiding place.

This fella, once had a protection racket on the dead man that the Sicilian was also a witness to. He pointed the police in the right direction and how to find him. The woman from the laundry shop said,

"Just follow the laundry that leaves the launderette on Clements road."

The police followed this laundry man, who had clean clothes for the Mafia Don, unbeknownst to him that the clothes were for him, and by doing this, he led the police, straight to the Don and he didn't even know it. The notes were all written in riddles anyway, but it was better to be safe than sorry. They had gone through great lengths to keep things as underground as possible. Even though the other mob Don was a recluse the police had still got him.

Grassing is the best information you can have in a case. When the grassing stops, the pathway becomes cold, but when those that have been caught keep talking, the pathway becomes hot and is then littered with bust after bust and result after result for the police. That's why these people worked in the way they did; to try and protect themselves and others involved within their Firm.

With every new technology and law that comes out, a new method or device comes out to break or beat them. If you wanted to get away with certain things in this game, then you had to play by the rules and work in this way, or you had to start thinking like a police officer. Otherwise you had no chance at all, no matter how crazy it seemed. It was paranoia yes, but paranoia was a great tool in this day and age with these sorts of players that we were now working with.

You didn't take risks or chances unless the risks were calculated. These people had the money and the man-power to do these sorts of things, to stay on top of their game. They would sweep buildings, hotels and restaurants before they had meetings in them. They would do the same to their cars and the taxis before they ride in them unless they had a new one every week by renting the cars.

They knew they were being bugged and watched most, if not all, of the time as they had ruffled a lot of feathers in regards to the authorities and the police. Killing the judge made them the public enemy and number one in the eyes of the police. The people they were corrupting would tell them so. So they would rent cars and hand them back every few days. The whole Sicilian family had thought a lot of Johnny and had heard plenty of good things about him and how he conducted himself and the lengths he had and would go to for all the Firms if asked.

You could see the fear in their enemies' eyes when his name was mentioned. To move in the same circle of business that they now all could do with each other was unheard of, but Johnny was and had been connected to them all. In all fairness it was Johnny that had made them all far more successful than they could have been alone. He had definitely opened a doorway for Mr Nice and the Sicilian mob and some of the Firms in South American and Mexico.

This meant they could now flood England and America with cocaine via Miami. The mob boss Mr Nice wanted to see Johnny as he had stuck to his word and wanted to give him his share of the money that he hoped he was due to receive on this meeting, or to put a contract out on him if he had done a runner with their money.

If he was there, he could pay what he was owed and now tell Johnny he had to be very careful, as his life was in danger, now the other family had found out he was connected to him and the police were hot on everyone's tails trying to do plea bargains with those that were going down!

He wanted to tell him that he was wanted to stand witness. He was on camera, which meant they would be soon snooping around him and his bank account unless he moved fast, but unbeknownst to the Sicilian boss, Johnny was already dead and would not be meeting him. He would now only be meeting Mr Nice.

CHAPTER 23

The Sicilian mobs family yacht cut through the very calm water towards the harbour, it began to slow down a bit as it juddered closer into the harbour mouth in Marbella. With each slight burst of the powerful listed engines, it pulsed through the water. It pushed and churned its way through in between the harbour walls, churning at the water turning it to froth. It glided forward a bit more with each blast before it finally came to a rest at the side of the harbour. With a quick growl from the engines and a last big shudder and a cough as the engines finally came to a resting stop. The yacht was silent, just sat there bobbing up and down on the ripples of the waves that lapped at the bottom of the boat.

The yacht had now moored up inside the harbour and rested next to the other yachts that had also come to rest. There were some really lush yachts parked up. Definitely, a few quid had been spent on them. How the other half live eh?

The crew scurried round to moor the yacht up. The anchor chain slowly fell and then speeded up as the anchor smashed through the surface of the clear water with a massive splash. Then it sank deep down to the bottom hitting the sea bed and came to a halt. Then the chain finished pouring out as it fell over the side of the boat. The yacht was shining as the sun rays shone down onto it. It glistened white like a pearl and reflected into the water while it sat there bobbing up and down slowly on the ripples of the clear blue Mediterranean Sea, while it lapped at the walls of the dock.

It was very excessive and was like a little floating hotel. It looked the bollocks. It had its own swimming pool and Jacuzzi. It was pure white with a silver trim that ran through the length of it. There was a speedboat hanging on a little crane on the back. It also had a casino on board as well and a little night club. It had blue lighting on the side of the bow with a picture of a flying Angel. It towered over the other boats, just to give you some idea of how big it was. It was proper luxurious. The yacht was turning more heads then in a tennis match, as it rested at the side of the harbour. People were staring at how plush it was and taking photos of it even though it was next to some other very nice and big yachts.

"Are you ready Mr Nice?" the crew captain asked.

Mr Nice looked up at Wong's face and smiled as he pushed the chess piece across the board.

"Checkmate Wong. Sorry my friend but if you snooze you lose. I thought you knew how to play chess after being banged up. You should be a wizard at it."

"That was many years ago."

Mr Nice then turned to the crew Captain. "Are you ready Sir?"

"I am now."

He swigged down the last bit of brandy from his glass and took a puff of his Cuban cigar and slowly let the smoke out.

"Grab the bags Wong."

"It's not checkmate Mr Nice," Wong said as Mr Nice stood up.

"That's what I like about you Wong, you never know when to stop even when you're fucked by my next move and it will be, there you go *check mate*. I take it you're back over here as things have gone wrong and you need my help again? I thought you were doing well with them DVDs you were copying?"

"Yes, things are still okay. I just have a few other things back in England I need to sort out Mr Nice."

Mr Nice patted him on the shoulder, "Don't worry my little prawn cracker, all will be okay. You'll see."

He then walked towards the stairs.

Wong stood up still studying the board for a chance but Mr Nice knew he had made sure there was no chance and that he had covered every angle possible and that it was indeed checkmate for Mr Wong, as he was ten moves ahead of him. He puts on his Armani shades and looked around. He did a button up on his jacket as it blew apart in the warm sea breeze. He looked left and right from the top of the yacht and followed Mr Nice to the stairs.

Mr Nice spotted who he was looking for as he focused on him. He could see Don F had arrived. Being so far away, Mr Nice wasn't too sure if it was him at first as it had been such a long time since he had met with him face to face. A lot had happened since then.

They had done business many times, but as they would use Johnny as the go-between, they rarely saw each other face-to-face. Johnny was always out there, helping the Sicilian Firm from time to time with their troubles. Mr Nice didn't want to get too involved directly and Mr Nice was now using his other henchman Malcolm to do business in England. Malcolm was now the new go-between and had known him for years and had virtually grown up with him.

Malcolm was now taking care of things for Mr Nice as Johnny was gone but he wasn't the same calibre of man as Johnny and was just running the drugs side of things, not the collecting. Now the cocaine field had been destroyed Malcolm was left over in England to run things in London. There was no need for him to be out in Spain looking after Mr Nice's empire and there was no need for Mr Nice to be in England after the close one at Mandy's funeral.

It was getting too risky for Mr Nice to be over there and he had vowed to himself he wouldn't come over to England again unless it was very, very necessary. Even to the Fat Cat Russian's organised underground fights. After all, he too would have been arrested at Mandy's funeral if he had attended but lucky for him, he was in Columbia! So to be safe he knew it was time to stay low for a change away from the police and they were closing in on him well in London.

Malcolm could come out here and go back as it wasn't a problem for him, but for Mr Nice it would soon release suspicion with the police investigations that would now be going on. Mr B and the others had been caught and we had all been seen at Mandy's funeral.

CHAPTER 24

"Come, Wong I think it's time I introduced you to some people I work with."

Wong was still trying to think of every move possible to get out of the inevitable checkmate he had now found himself in.

"There's someone I'd like you to meet." They walked along the boat and down the steps to the lower deck of the yacht. Wong was carrying two rather small cases. They wheeled along behind him. He had caught up and was walking next to Mr Nice.

They both thanked the crew then walked casually down towards the front of the boat. Wong had the money and no one else knew that. To everyone else, it just looked like he was a holiday maker carrying his bags. They didn't know that £250,000 was stashed in the bags and had just been transported to Marbella. Wong was holding onto the bags very tightly as walked off the boat and caught up with Mr Nice. That's where they were met by Don F and his Russian bodyguard.

The Sicilian boss was leaning with crossed arms on

a black BMW MX5 Jeep. As Mr Nice and Wong walked closer they could see he was well dressed in a black suit with a white shirt underneath. Don F was waiting with his arms folded and legs crossed; sitting there casually leant against the BMW Jeep. He watched Mr Nice and Wong moving towards them as they came closer to him.

The bodyguard had his hands by his side, watching everyone's move. He was weighing them both up with his studying glance and staring eyes. He was very alert and on the ball. As Wong and Mr Nice approach the Sicilian boss, he leaned away from the Jeep and stood up straight. He unfolded his arms as they approached him. He was a very smart and well-groomed man.

You could tell by the way he looked. But, being as he had just got out the nick, he was looking a little rough around the edges from his usually well-groomed self. His hair was in need of a trim and he could do with a manicure. He was well switched on and seemed like a no nonsense sort of fella. I guess that's why he was who he was.

"Please, remove your glasses Mr Nice. Men who wear shades have something to hide in their eyes and can become very untrustworthy. You can tell where a man's heart is if you can look deep into his eyes, and I want to see the fear before I smell it. You can see if they are concentrating on what I am telling them. A lot of people I talk to I may as well be pouring water on a duck's back. It goes in one ear and out the other. I want to see in your eyes and that you are acknowledging everything I'm about to tell you and the same with others as then if I can see the whites of their eyes I know there will be no mistakes with the instructions I give them. I can study their soul and know they are listening to me very carefully and aren't going to miss something I have said that is deadly important to me, my family and the contacts it concerns. You know what I mean Mr Nice? I don't want anyone to miss a thing as they may mess up later on while they still work for me. When the shit hits the fan, as you English say, they can't say, '*Well you didn't say that bit,*' as I will know I had. So, it makes it a lot easier once I pull the trigger or something terrible may happen to them. I will know deep in my heart that they deserved everything they got when they hit the floor. Dead! So there's no need for tears."

He spoke slowly but precisely and every word spoken was very wise and made perfect sense to those who it was being spoken to.

Mr Nice took off his glasses. Wong looked at Mr Nice like the fella was a bit nuts unsure whether he was taking the piss. Either that or he was doing too much cocaine. He dropped the cases in front of the Sicilian mob boss.

"I take it these are yours."

Don F came across as a bit of a nutter. They all were in this game when they reach the top. You wouldn't have a clue that they were and that's the way they liked it. That's why they stayed at the top for as long as they did. Some people thought they were at the top but believe me, they were not. They were just pawns used in a bigger chess game.

"I see you like our yacht Mr Nice?"

"Yes, very nice. I could get used to travelling like this."

"Well, if you stick with us, you just might."

The bodyguard checked Wong but not Mr Nice for bugs or weapons. The boss then stood forward and kissed Mr Nice on both sides of his check, then cuddled him.

"It's great to see you after so long. Okay before we get into my Jeep, let's talk. It's best we walk and talk at the same time as the Jeep could be bugged for all I know. You can never be too careful now Mr Nice. The authorities have told the locals that if they grass us up for our extortion rackets, they will be immune from the local government tax. Can you believe it?"

He laughed before continuing, "And they are now being encouraged to grass on us or give info about our work. That's why a lot of my family and others have been caught and the others in other families too and they think it's us so they play ball with the police. The businesses in Sicily and other places have grown sick of paying our protection money, even though we have had others that don't want to pay killed or hurt or have destroyed their businesses as promised. Things are changing fast Mr Nice. The world is now a crazy place. It's dog eat dog my friend and if you haven't got the dogs, then you're stuck with the pussies and you'll be dead very soon or banged up. The mayor of Ragusa has made a ruling; anyone co-operating with the cops will be immune from their local tax. So it's sad to say Mr Nice but things have started to come on top for all in Sicily, no matter how connected they once were. Things are changing now with regards to the businesses we run and more so now a judge has been killed by the nicking of the main boss in Sicily. It means we must be careful with everything we do. I have asked for you to come here and not to Sicily to sort out this little thing I have asked of you and to update you on events that have happened. Have you heard from Johnny?"

"No."

"I had to ask it of you to come here as I haven't been able to make contact with Johnny. I hope you didn't mind and I know there are other matters we can sort out now you're out here."

"I see," said Mr Nice.

"Tell me Mr Nice. Where are Johnny and Mandy?"

"Well they are both dead."

"*What*?"

"Yes, both killed. Mandy by the Colombian Cartel and Johnny by the police in England."

"That's dreadful news."

"We can't take any chances now. Things are going wrong, or seem to be, on both sides of the waters," Don F mused. He said it was a shame to lose Johnny as he would have taken anyone out of the game and was very loyal and did what was asked of him with no questions asked and it's hard to find people who can walk the walk and talk the talk at the same time. "There's not many people out there like that, but he would only do it on my say so." Mr Nice said.

"Of course."

"There are so many people out here, as you know Mr Nice, that promise you the world but when the time comes, you end up with fuck all. They're all just full of false promises and all they work off is false hope."

"Johnny did do a lot of work for you."

"I understand he also did a lot for my family members. I thought it was unknown to most people what he did for my family and me."

Johnny had done a few hits for the mob directly allegedly. He and the Sicilian mob boss had found out where the buried money was from the Asians and that was the last job they had done.

The Sicilian boss continued.

"I hear rumours that the police have found out now that we had the Asian Firm hit in Manchester and they tried to arrest you for it?"

"Yes that's right. I was nearly banged up for it because they found one of my cigars there in the underground car park."

"Well, let me tell you something Mr Nice … the police will soon be arresting me again as I'm now their key witness to another murder that my brother was involved with and I was there when a Sicilian Mafia judge was shot outside the courtroom that I had gone to for a trial on a murder that my brother was put up for. The police said they could do a deal and if I stood trial on the judge killer they would then drop the charge of murder on my brother to manslaughter. After all he only killed another rival mob member so I have to do it for him. They want me to stand trial on the case as I'm their one and only witness with regards to this judge being killed, but it means I will have to be put on witness protection. The other families will not approve of me helping out he police but it will help save my brother going down for murder. But it also means the police will see how much money I have been saving in a bank out here."

There was a pause before the Sicilian boss continued, "I will stand witness to try and get my brother off, but it means they will then be looking in to my accounts and take what is there, and it will mean my life will be in danger from then on from rival members of the family my brother had killed. Not to mention others that I work with. It's not good practice as you know to be doing deals with the police Mr Nice. I know I can trust you and that's why I have told you. So, they will be putting me on witness protection once they get me but I have been trying to avoid them as I need to sort this money out first because once they do get me, they will freeze my accounts and take all my assets. They know it's from the proceeds of crime, no matter how clean I can make it look. So, now you know why this money you have is important to me as no one else knows about it apart from us here. Thanks again for collecting it for me. You do have it don't you?"

"Yes we have it."

"That's good, I thought Johnny might have got to it first. Everyone in the Firm thought Johnny was just relaxing on holiday out there enjoying the sights when he was alive. Or that's what Johnny had made out, but he was out there working and doing what he did best for the Sicilian mob and the money he was making from these little jobs was going back to Mr Nice so that Johnny could be included in other matters and now it would have been the cocaine field. Johnny was out in Sicily making sure people were in body bags for them when he was alive and had been out here according to the Sicily job. The money the Sicilian mob was paying for his work would come over to you Mr Nice. All safe and sound on a Weston Union through the exchange next to Wong's restaurant. Ready for Wong to access to you from Johnny."

"I thought you were just being generous."

"Ha Ha. Generous? No. Smart? Yes."

"I knew you were looking after Johnny's money and the bar he bought when he was on the run as he had phoned me."

That's how the Sicilian mob knew about the Colombian field that Mr Nice was involved with.

Mr Nice would get paid money or a share in some other business for the jobs Johnny would do without really knowing it was from the mob as money was moving around quickly and he thought it was the drugs that they were paying over the odds for, not knowing that Johnny's bit was being added to it so that he could get more back when he needed it or buy in to the right venture like the Colombian field.

He would have made a few pounds extra on their investments, or that's what he was told by Mr Nice, not knowing that Johnny had also been hired out by the Sicilian mob and that half the money was going to Mr Nice for a safe return to Johnny. Once he split it with him in return for a share of twenty per cent of all the money made from his bar but now he was gone and Old School was running it meant Old School was now paying Mr Nice twenty percent of all the profits made on the bar.

It was all Mr Nice's money now Johnny and Mandy were gone. Mr Nice thought they were just gifts from the mob for doing well and making more money on the cocaine deals and cannabis and lorry runs, not really knowing that they were in fact payments for Johnny's handy work. But it all made sense now to Mr Nice. Once Don F started talking more and more openly about Johnny, he was really laying all his card out on the table, all in front of Mr Nice he knew his time had come and gone now. The Old Bill had their tentacles well into him and, he had let them trap him in to becoming a key witness in their case.

Johnny had done this last job for him; the killing of the two Asian bods in Manchester for the Sicilian mob for the stolen money that was Mr Nice's in the first place. The Sicilian mob man thought he was being smart by using Mr Nice's stolen money to buy a share in his field but the tables had turned and he was now stuck with the police.

The Sicilian mob man had told Mr Nice.

"I told Johnny that I would pay him half of this money when we met. He had said he would then share it with you for a share in the cocaine field that you have control of. So that's the story or the bare bones of it Mr Nice of how this money come about. I will give you half the money here back for twenty-five per cent stake in your field."

"What field?"

"Your field Mr Nice. The field you have control off in Colombia."

"Had." Mr Nice said.

"Had?"

The Mafia boss looked at Mr Nice funnily.

"Yes, had. It has all been destroyed."

"How di …"

Mr Nice interrupted.

"The interception eradicator team found it working for the police and government found out about it and have sprayed it all and while they were there they also upturned the two labs that we were using to turn the leaves into cocaine and now it's come on top. I think it had something to do with some deal that went a bit pear-shaped with some marine I had working with me. The Colombian dad whose daughter I was seeing didn't want to get involved in the drugs way of life any more after all he has four hotels now from the stuff. Why would he need to? So it is no longer any use to any one now. I have been working with other members of your family he lied as he still had the 40 keys and the South Americans and a German fella and people in Amsterdam to sort more cocaine out I'm waiting on it. That's why the rest of my cocaine was running low. The last 20 keys I sorted out to get a pilot to bring over it seems has got lost, so I sent the rest over by lorry to my friend's shipping yard out here in Spain but we now need to get it to England somehow but the German is working on it. So then there was no need for me to stay in Colombia once that had happened." Mr Nice had told only half of the truth.

He left out that he had a chance to steal a hundred keys

without anyone knowing so he took the opportunity to do so and so far had gotten away with it. Well, some of it as the rest has got nicked and he was just about to hand over the money from it to the Sicilian mob, not knowing that it was his own money.

It's thanks to Johnny. Things had quietened down and there was peace once again with most of them. The Sicilian boss was very grateful for Johnny's help and Mr Nice's and he now wanted to show his appreciation.

The Sicilian mob boss opened the bags after looking in one of them, then zipped the bag back up passed one of the bags back to Mr Nice.

"Here thanks for all your help." Mr Nice had deserved the money. After all he had arranged Johnny for them and got Johnny to do their dirty work with members of his family, even though it had now come on top for him. But that was his own fault. The money Johnny should had got for this work in Manchester for the Sicilian mob, he would have wanted Mandy to have but now they weren't around it would go to Mr Nice as Mr Nice had become his close family. Johnny had done this and some of his own work behind Mr Nice's back as he had now found out from Don F.

Mr Nice thought he would use this meeting as a good chance to sort out the finance matters with the Sicilian boss and also, he thought while he was here and that things were all good and he had now earned a few brownie points by doing this little favour for him. He thought it was a good time to ask him for the outstanding money for the shipment of cocaine that his son had dropped off before he had been caught and had gone down at the Old Bailey.

The money for it and for other business they had done which Mr Nice had organised was long overdue to him but still hadn't been paid for. He wanted it now so their money could be cleaned and used in London. One of them was in charge of cleaning certain money by putting their money through the fairgrounds and the horses.

It also went through underground card games and fights just to try and clean it up for them and keep the money moving and out to Geneva and Switzerland and into Bulgaria and then back in to Brussels through Prague. He was due a cut of that too and was due to get paid before the main boss got nicked, he hadn't seen or heard anything from this side until now. So he was due a few quid for his help from them.

Wong got into the Jeep after throwing the bags of cash into the boot and waited for them as they walked on. He was told to wait there by the Sicilian mob boss.

"This will only take a few seconds."

Wong looked at Mr Nice, very unsure about things. He could sense this man was very important and had the important air of confidence about him that Wong had only seen from Mr Nice. But now the Sicilian man was overpowering even Mr Nice's confidence a little. You just knew you had to do as you were told as you knew it wasn't worth arguing as men with money were dangerous and looking at the yacht they had a lot more than Wong and Mr Nice put together for now. A man that can just give away half of £250,000 like that didn't mess about. It wasn't like the fellas back home giving it this and that and talking bollocks, promising you the world and coming up with their thumb up their arse. This man talked business. Otherwise he wouldn't talk to you at all. Mr Nice nodded and walked ahead with the Sicilian man and the bodyguard in tow back up towards the yacht.

"Mr Nice … It's very sad Johnny is no longer with us …"

"Yes. Very sad …"

"In this life death is one thing every man shall face and for some it comes around quicker than others in this game. Quicker than you might think Mr Nice. Every day that goes past there could be a bullet with your name on it. You make more enemies than friends in this life. Or a freak accident could be set up that you might be involved with … That's why you must hold all your cards close to your chest and try and stay out the lime light. I tell you this for your own safety Mr Nice with regards to the things that are now happening around me.

"On the meeting you had in the Grosvenor hotel in Mafia a few months back - I think you were staying there as you were attending some underground fight - you met with my cousin that owned the hairdressers. He said that you wanted some money for a job lot of cocaine your son got caught with that was going to my friend that works in the coffee shop in London on Wardour Street. I was told when he passed the message to me and I was going to sort it out before all this had happened."

"Haven't you had enough of my money?" Mr Nice asked.

"I just would like what is owed to me. Nothing more, nothing less. So I can pay all involved in the last six shipments that we had arranged and get back some of what was lost coming over from the field as a pilot of mine had lost a shipment. I haven't been paid for those shipments yet and like I said, once the main boss had been caught, everyone has cut their ties and the next thing no money is changing hands then next thing I know a lot of good contacts and good people are going down. Then I get the call from your wife in Manchester to come and help you out."

"I understand your concern and I know you just want everything above board and paid off. That's not a problem Mr Nice. With big money comes big responsibility and a lot more stress. As I'm sure you well know. After being able to call the shots as being an owner of a Colombian field, you understand how things work. Not many get to the top of the food chain like yourself and live to tell the tale Mr Nice. Mr Nice you're not thinking of breaking your connections with us for good now Johnny is gone are you? As that's what it seems to me. After all we have all earned each other a great deal of money and you have shown us where your responsibility lies by doing this little favour for me. My family and I like that. Even if you are now working close with the South Americans without our consent. My family have decided to let you have the money that you are owed."

The Sicilian boss was lying. He knew the police were on to him he needed someone he trusted to be able to get it back at a later stage.

"We will give you the money. As a token of all the hard work you and Johnny have shown my family in the past and out of respect and loyalty to Johnny. I will hand all money owed over to you and I would like to make sure you get it personally ... So would the rest of my family, but others are not so sure about it. We are very grateful for you and for Johnny's help. As without that help we could not operate on the scale we have all been able to enjoy and with your North American connection. Things have gone well, but like all good things they soon come to an end. Not only are we battling with our enemies we are now also battling with the authorities that get closer and closer to us every day, and our activities as you know or may not. We have had to take measures to get our money in the banks without questions.

Well not too many … Now certain people are out of the way there is peace … In my garden … In Sicily my children play in the garden without fear of bullets coming from people who seek revenge. It has been done all undercover of Johnny and they don't know it came from us directly. This is why they can no longer point the finger of blame and, most importantly, retaliate anything to us. If you don't know the enemy Mr Nice how can you get to it? The question I would like to ask you is this Mr Nice, who is more dangerous the gangster or his runner?"

"Mmm," Mr Nice replied as he contemplated the question. He felt a bit off guard by it as he knew that Johnny had made it possible for most of these things to happen.

"So, all this is thanks to you for the little favours your man Johnny had done for you and in turn us. So my father has granted the money for you that is owed and a little extra from our account out here in Marbella."

"Thank you," said Mr Nice.

"This is why I have asked you to come over here too," the Sicilian lied, "So I can repay the favours by giving you the money you have earned and of course to see you once again and to get the money dug up and to see if Johnny had crossed me. I am proved wrong again by men of loyalty. As it has shown through once again. Money Mr Nice. Anyone with half a brain can make a few quid. It's been a long time and we were much younger back then. When things were as good as they were then with the Cartel. Come, let's go. I shall take you to our bank and give you what is rightfully yours."

They then went back to the Jeep.

The Sicilian mob boss turned to Wong.

"I don't know you … But I'm sure if Mr Nice has brought you this close to us that means you are trusted with many things that concern Mr Nice."

"Yes he is," said Mr Nice.

"Nice to meet you." Wong put out his hand as the Sicilian mob boss turns round and Wong looks at Mr Nice as Mr Nice comforts him and pulls out a cigar.

The Sicilian told the bodyguard to drive for a bit towards the bank all the time not realising the white van which was presently out of sight was following them.

CHAPTER 25

Mr Nice thought it was a good time to look at some properties whilst he was out here and now he was due to get a lot of money, it was a good time to catch up on business with Wong. It had been ages since their last get together, that's why Mr Nice invited him here with him after Mandy's funeral and the underground fight. Mr Nice liked Marbella and felt comfortable out here. Now that everything was out in the open and everything would soon be put to rest with the Sicilian mafia, he would be paid and that would be a closed page for them and the Colombians. He wouldn't want to go back there just in case it comes to light about the hundred keys.

Once that was all over in England then that too would be another chapter closed and he would be his own boss. He could then worry about his own problems and not about other peoples. He was really interested in buying a new villa with this new money that was coming his way. Now Johnny was gone, it was now all his and, coming from the Sicilian mob, it would be already clean so he wouldn't have the stress or mess of having to get it all cleaned himself.

He wanted a change and a much needed one too. He himself had already walked from court on a charge in Spain, which had been set up and fabricated to make it look like he had done it. This was the murder of the farmer, the one the police had found in England that had sold the cocaine to the Asian fellas, the ones it turned out Johnny had killed in the underground car park and the police had said Mr Nice had overseen it if not done it himself.

The police had tried to charge Johnny but as he was dead, they tried their utmost to charge Mr Nice for it. The police didn't have the evidence they needed and they couldn't make this one stick. The case against him had collapsed, which was very embarrassing for them. The authorities wanted him so badly they tried and tried all sorts of measures to get a charge that would stick on him but when the time came, when they did think they had him bang to rights, he walked from court-walked with a big smile on his face.

Even though they had planted it all on him and had found a cigar with his DNA on it at the scene. Well, it was the one he had given to Johnny. The same one that had been found in his place in Spain but like Mr Nice said: *Everyone I know smokes these cigars and they are well liked throughout the underworld. So it could be any one of us.*

He was right, the Judge had to concede and after Mr Nice confirmed he had been to the underground car park five weeks ago to collect his car but the real reason was to bet in a underground fight that took place there with a friend of Wong's and some Fat Cat Russian before they had gone to Mandy's funeral. Of course this explained why Johnny knew the car park and was there to call the meeting with the Asian brothers.

The Judge was very upset with Mr Nice walking and so was the England judicial system and Scotland Yard as they also thought they had him. But the evidence against him was so flimsy there was no way a conviction could be made. The English Judge was happier to learn that Mr Nice was in custody and could be going down.

He was in close talks with the Spanish judge, but the long and short of it was, that Mr Nice was walking free once again at the tax payer's expense. The police too were hoping that he would go down for this and put an end to the surveillance work but this time they really did have the wrong man. So the police had missed their chance and wasted the courts and everyone else's time involved in the case. The police and the crown had tried so hard to desperately bring Mr Nice to justice and everyone around him connected to his empire, but they had failed and now they needed a new lead as Johnny was gone. The Chief of Police wasn't impressed when Mr Nice's top solicitor had found a loophole in their case and had exposed them for the attempted set up.

On this little piece of substantial evidence against him, it didn't look too good once it came out in court that they had tried to set him up and had done things above and beyond the law without getting the correct authorised action to do certain things or follow the correct procedures that they should have done; like bugging his phone. They should have taken the right procedure to get the information they needed for the case and not just go on circumstantial evidence and hearsay. Then they may have realised that Mr Nice was talking about something else and not what the police had stumbled on, which was a message on his phone which they then made their arrest on.

The message had said, *Make it happen. I don't care just let him have it*, and this is what they tried to build the crumbling case around, that message and the cigar found at the scene of the crime. The Chief of Police was supremely vexed with how this had panned out and was almost catatonic with rage when the Judge had a 'quiet word' with him and 'suggested' he stop wasting time and resources on Mr Nice and to concentrate his efforts on finding the weakest link within his Firm.

"Then you might get him and all of them if you're lucky. I will not condone you bending the law to catch him. Even though it was him that had given the orders. If you had waited and done everything by the book he would now be behind bars. Now get out my office and catch some crooks. No more fuck ups. Otherwise, you'll be on foot patrol like the rest of them and I'll be making a note with all the details to the Home Office about all this."

The Chief of Police then got it in the neck from The Spanish Judge who was also involved in this complex caper, "I want everything done by the book from now on. With this new evidence from the English judge, we can't afford any more mess ups. Do you hear me? If you want these behind bars, then do it right and we will have them all."

"Yes."

"If you want results then get the Sicilian boss and the rest of the family on witness protection and get him to testify and then get the money they are holding in the bank. Arrest the Sicilian mob boss for his own safety, then we will be getting somewhere."

Don F reported to Mr Nice that the word on the streets was that things were going from bad to worse and the police were now on the mob's tail faster than the paparazzi. This should and could be their last meeting for everyone's safety as they wouldn't want to get nicked just for the association.

"I do know a lot of my Firm have been arrested and others in other Firms too have gone down. Even my uncle is on a case for murder," Don F continued, "It looks like the mob are going down. The police now want me, so I'm told, as I'm the key witness in a case for my uncle and my life is in danger. Someone had turned super grass and has been opening up to the police about all my affairs, causing others to get nicked. Also about money we have in different banks and places." *I understand* Mr Nice thought to himself as he nodded his assent.

A new Villa in a new place meant a new start to this drug empire. If the Sicilian mob were going down, that meant there was a hole in the market that he could fill. Mr Nice had now created an empire he wanted for himself and was now making it bigger by the day. Now the Sicilian mob were shutting up shop for their own protection. With others lying low from the police it meant he could be at liberty to make as much money as he could without any problems or anyone or other Firms getting in the way.

This would be done all undercover with Malcolm at the helm. Malcolm was a people person and could mix in all circles of life. Mr Nice would use him to hide behind and do his work all safe and sound in England or wherever needed. It also meant Mr Nice would have England well sewn up even though he would settle in Marbella. The life Mr Nice once had as small-time crime crook in London running a few security Firms and clubs and scams here, there and everywhere; like lead coins bent twenty pound notes, copied credit cards, porn movies, underground fights and bookie scams and other misdemeanours that he was well involved with, had now been left behind him and was now onto a winner.

After meeting with Johnny and getting involved with the Colombians and their daughter, he had hit the jackpot by contacting these people. He was now rubbing shoulders with the Sicilian mobs directly again, thanks to Johnny. Out here he could continue to be the ruthless businessman he always knew he was, without anyone knowing the real nature of his or their business and without anyone really knowing his connection and bringing attention to himself for the police to follow.

He hoped by doing this they would soon bring their investigation to a halt as there wouldn't be much to report on so the Sicilian mob and they wouldn't be under the watchful eyes of people also if he was out here he would be out of the way from his enemies who would be ready to grass him up and bring him down at any given chance like what had seemed to have happened to the Sicilian mob.

Malcolm anticipated his moves and the moves of his drug trade. He was the conductor and they were his bands men. The less people who knew about Mr Nice and his business the better, so by using Malcolm as the front line man he would eventually go unnoticed, living it large in a new villa he was going to buy with the new money he was due to get.

He wanted to be out of the limelight from now on as advised by the Sicilian mob as it was getting close with the police pulling them in; he had been there seen it and done it all so why not stay out of the limelight and let someone else take the risks for once? It was time to be very careful. The police were on everyone's case and were closing in fast by the sounds of what he had heard from the Sicilian boss and himself walking free from court with no case to answer.

He knew they wanted him and wanted him bad. Marbella seemed like a nice place. The people were all friendly and there were loads of ex-villains living out there. So, for Mr Nice it would be home from home. It would be a lot easier for Mr Nice to conduct his empire here, without drawing too much of the wrong type of attention to himself and the rest of the Firms he was now involved with. No one would see the Firm come and go if he could buy a villa that had its own bit of private beach that backed onto the back, as this would mean Firms could come straight from the sea and land on his bit of the beach with no dramas and out of the way of prying eyes.

Once he had the money to buy it outright he would, and that day coming sooner then he thought. He could rent the one out he had in the other part of Spain or just sell it off to the Marine Brett's Old Man who was already interested in Johnny's bar out in Barbados.

So, Don F agreed that Mr Nice could have access to some of their funds that were being stored in the mobs' account out here. After all, he had earned them. Well, Johnny had and they still owed Mr Nice for the last shipment that had been sent. Don F took him to the bank. The bank manager embraced Don F as one would a brother. When he walked into the bank one of the managers came and kissed him on each side of his face and said,

"Many thanks for all your help." He then shook Mr Nice's hand. Just picture the scene two made men as menacing as hell rocking up to a bank. They both bowled into the bank and were given priority. As soon as both men and the bodyguard walked in, the good looking clerks all looked up and smiled and one waved. They all knew or thought they knew what they were all about.

The employees of the bank thought he bought and sold off businesses for that's what the manager had told them. The air of money can speak several languages to many people. If you show people that have a few quid, people treat you in weird and wonderful ways and it can make some women's eyes fill with hearts like in the cartoons when they see how many zeros are on the end of your account. Not all men and women of course.

Don F was a very rich man indeed and Mr Nice was about to become likewise as privileged. The police knew it and they thought they would be able to get their hands on the Sicilian boss's money themselves as once he was on witness protection the money would go to the police once they had him in their protective custody for the case they were working on with regards to the killing of the judge and he was being made to stand witness for his own safety.

He knew they would be taking the money he had worked for nearly five years and he wouldn't be able to explain it to them so it was as good as gone. The police knew this and so did the Sicilian mob man, so he had to act first. Mr Nice was about to get a lot richer and the bank knew it. They had seen the zeros on the end of the mobs boss's bank account as he now wanted to transfer the lot to Mr Nice in the hope he could get some of it back at a later stage, unbeknown to Mr Nice, as he had been tipped off that he would soon be arrested and made to stand trial on the case his uncle was involved with and the killing of the judge. He knew they would lay him bare and would seize all his assets and he, knew that by them doing this, his life would be in danger. So, transferring the money to Mr Nice was part of the plan, unbeknown to anyone else, and definitely not Mr Nice. It was going to be a smart move on the Sicilian mob's part.

The bank manager was pleased to see them. Well I would be happy to see him too if I was in his shoes being paid a nice fee to keep his dirty money in my account for a small percentage back. The story was, the bank manager's daughter nearly got raped by this man at outside a nightclub. She had bitten his hand and ran off. It was caught on CCTV. She managed to break free and the fella was arrested. The police put him on remand as he had done this sort of thing before but the police said he would probably get a year or so or may get off with a warning. The bank manager did not like this. After all he could have raped his daughter. What if he had raped and hurt her? So he wanted to him hurt back.

The bank manager not being happy with the police went to his friend, even though he had got a three month prison sentence. He wanted to sort it out his own way. So he had a chat with one of his friends who then had turned to Don F. The friend of the bank manager knew the Sicilian mobs boss's brother. He said he wanted him done, meaning hurt. They said it was possible. He asked how much it cost and he was told one thousand pounds. Don F had asked what the man who wanted the man hurt did for a living and they were told he was a big bank manager in Marbella. So, once they knew he was a bank manager to one of the biggest banks in Marbella the Sicilian mob boss said they would do it for free for him and come to an arrangement later once the deed was done. Don F said he would get it so he had phoned and got a hit man out on this fella that had done the deed. While he was in prison he was shot dead in the prison grounds whilst he had been let out on occasion by the prison guards. He had been shot by Johnny for them, as the Sicilian mob's hit man had been arrested now for the drive-by killing of the judge in Sicily. The mob boss had asked Johnny do it at short notice and he did, which meant he had scored big points this time round for the Sicilian mob. Once the hit was done for the bank manager, the mob's dirty money came flying into the bank with no questions asked.

So when the Sicilian man and Mr Nice came into the vault of the bank Mr Nice said,

"As easy as that?"

"No it's not." The Sicilian mob boss said.

A call was made to someone then the phone was given to the bank manager and then the bank manager gave the phone back to the mob boss. Mr Nice was then asked to sign some and then he was added to the bank account as the benefactor to the money and the Sicilian man was taken off.

The bank manager told Mr Nice that the money was ready or would be ready within two days for Mr Nice to access. Or he could transfer it if he wanted to. It could then go through to any business he wanted in London with no questions asked. All he would need to do is sign for it once it reached where it had been sent to. It could then be transferred to Wong's restaurant and hidden in his basement if need be.

Yang would receive it on behalf of Wong from the exchange next to Wong's restaurant in China town. Even though she was a woman, she didn't mess about and was very loyal to Wong and would do whatever he had asked of her so she would go and collect money for him if and once it had been sent over from wherever it was sent from to the exchange Mr Nice thought then it would be transferred into Wong's bank account with a bent lawyer. It was Yang's name on the restaurants deeds and Wong's restaurant was right next to the exchange, which made it easier to ship money to the mainland and then back out to Guernsey.

Yang could slip out, put on a suit and then she was ready to go in and out of the exchange without any problems. She collected the money and pushed it on to other sources that Mr Nice would need it to go to. That's if Mr Nice wanted it transferred there. Wong would sometimes take it out of the country to the mainland himself. Yang had protected Wong many times. There was once a time when these fellas came into Wong's restaurant and had told him to hand over his cocaine. They had pulled guns on him, she had stepped in the way and disarmed them both as Wong looked up and laughed and said to the gangsters:

"You look more like pranksters to me." She then stabbed them both with the chop sticks that had her hair tied up. She then sold the bodies for spare parts on the black market to the shop next door. As Wong laughed, she smiled and put the guns down the sides of her clothes. She was a deadly assassin, hired by Wong as she was wanted over in China for accessory to murder. Two murders in fact; for some rich Chinese businessmen.

She was sleeping with someone who was dealing in large quantities of heroin. Wong had met her and looked after her here in London while she was on the run. He had met her in a brothel as she was making a porno behind a two way mirror at the brothel house he went in to he had clocked it as he saw the door open a little and washed himself before he went in with the working girl and had sex. He had gone mad after sleeping with the working girl and then kicked the door open to see her sitting there with a movie camera making homemade porn videos.

"Where's the tape?"

"Here."

She had told him what she was about and why she was

there after they had a little fight and he had got the better of her as he had caught her off guard. She had told him she needed money and need to stay out of the way of trouble for a bit.

"Look, making porno films in some backstreet brothel isn't going to pay you much," he said. "Come and work for me"

Wong had head-butted the maid, who was shouting at him in Chinese to get out while the other working girl was screaming.

"Come, I will look after you."

She then came to work for him as his minder. He would pay her much better than what she was getting filming homemade pornos at a secret hidey-hole in a brothel. She was quite good looking herself too but very fiery and hard as nails, which Wong liked.

Mr Nice could now have access to this money when and where he needed it. He could now buy the property he liked out in Marbella. The banks solicitors said the only bad thing was it had to be in his name. Until the money changed hands then it could be put in any name of his choice. Mr Nice didn't trust anyone else and he already had so much of his money in other peoples' accounts and he had run out of people he could ask to hold onto it.

"If I had got this much respect going into the bank back in the day then I wouldn't have bothered wearing a balaclava and I would have left the tools in the car and wouldn't have bothered bringing them in with me. A few kisses on the side of the cheek and then a handshake and the manager would be on his knees opening the safe for me. Job done! All I would have to do is put the contents into my bags no problems shake his hand again and be gone." Mr Nice joked and they all laughed.

Don F explained that to get the money in there without a paper trail was very hard.

"We had to convince the other bank manager, it wasn't easy even though he owed me a big favour. I guess having the gun to his head helped," he smiled, "It may all look easy to you Mr Nice but believe me a lot of people have had to do as they are told for us to be able to walk into the bank like we fucking own this Island. Do you understand me? As with all large amounts of dirty cash comes a large amount of organising and the correct people to make sure things look like it is all above board. When clearly it isn't as you now can see. Mr Nice, the question is always where did the money come from in the first place? If you can't answer that, then you're in big trouble. That's the question that everyone gets stuck with when asked by the authorities about bent money. If you can answer that one with confidence, then you're one of the people who has made it and made it big. Very big my friend, and if your that big, you will have made a lot of unwanted attention and some bad enemies too. That goes with making money. In this way of life, as you know it's not all champagne and cocaine, a lot of people have to get hurt."

They then left the bank, thanked the manager and went back to the café as they had left Wong there waiting for them to return.

"It was nice to meet you gentlemen," Don F said, "And once again a pleasure to see you Mr Nice. Thanks for coming through with the money."

"Not a problem. A man's word is his word," Mr Nice said in grave mock honourable tones, "If Johnny was here he would have delivered just as you did. I thought I could always trust you but you never can tell. Even the biggest of men have doubts and get burnt a few times, even after so long." The two men then embraced kissing each other on the side of their cheeks. Don F then turned to Wong. "Take care my friend. It's the men behind us that make us stand strong and it's always the gangster's runner that's more dangerous my friend. Remember that."

He got in to his BMW X5 with his minder and drove off.

Mr Nice sat down and ordered a latté coffee. He noticed that a white van had also pulled off out of an alleyway, and now seemed to be following the Sicilian mob boss's Four By Four. Mr Nice tried to ring him as the coffee was placed onto the table, but he got no answer. So, he picked up his cup and looked on as he had a sip and spat it out again as before you knew it the van was ramming the Italian man's BMW X5.

It swerved to miss an oncoming truck and crashed through the barriers, then disappeared for a bit. Then all of a sudden it flipped up and flew off the road and collided with the rocks below and blew up on impact as it came to rest at the bottom. Mr Nice and Wong couldn't believe what they had seen. Everyone else in the café also saw as they stood up and looked all concerned with what they had just witnessed and what had now looked like an accident. Then the men in the van said,

"Shit, now we have fucked it."

They got out and looked down and phoned the Judge.

"It's done sir. The minder is dead but he is now with us."

"Did it look like an accident?"

"Yes it looked like an accident."

Before they had rammed the Four By Four off the road they had pulled it over and had pulled the gangsters out and had flashed their badges to show they were police. He then had shot the minder as the mob boss had done a deal with the police unbeknown to everyone and he was now on witness protection for his own safety. The police wanted the money in the bank, not knowing that he had signed it over and that he had outsmarted them. Now it was signed over to Mr Nice. Some quick thinking on his behalf, but to everyone he was now dead but really he had passed the money on and not let the police get it in the hope of reclaiming his money another time.

He was free now and on police protection. Soon he would have a new identity and would be living somewhere nice again. If he had to help them with their enquiries he would tell them about Johnny as he was now dead it didn't matter. He would have been the winner in the long run as he now knew the money was safe and the police couldn't stop it.

"Ok let's get the money now."

"It's not in my name sir." Don F told the judge calmly once the police had bought him to them.

The police officer was told to take him to the bank.

"Okay so where's the money?" the Judge asked on the phone to his right, "That wasn't what we had arranged, was it?" The voice shouted down the phone. "How is he supposed to sign the money to us now? You should have got him to sign it over to you and arrested him in the bank."

"Christ, this operation had gone to shit," the Officer retorted, "I wanted to see who the other man who went into the bank with him was."

The Judge sighed, he couldn't really fault that reasoning, and,

"Well did you see him? Now with any luck it will be this man the English authorities call the Milkman."

"Leave it with me."

They got back in their van and quickly drove off.

The Judge phoned his pal in the police force and told them to hit the bank after they had now known the money was definitely in there, but they now had no access to it. It wasn't in the name of the Sicilian mob boss anymore. They had done the deal with him; as long as the money was released to them as the surveillance team had followed them all and had all the info now but didn't know it had been signed over just yet to Mr Nice. It was definitely a smart bit of thinking by Don F and had saved the money. *Now it was due to Mr Nice* the mob boss thought. The police had sent their police information into getting him to sign for the money but the bank refused it, saying he was not the benefactor of it and didn't know why he was here.

So, the police knew the manager had to also been in on it, but how? He was refused by the bank manager and also the Sicilian mob boss was too. He wrote his signature down for the police and for the managers but the bank manger just shook his head.

"Sorry sir. This account has not been verified by this signature anymore. A new benefactor has now been put in place."

"Who is this?"

"Sorry, I can't tell you that."

"Okay." The informer shows his badge.

"It's a wealthy Londoner sir. I can't give you any more than that. Only a contact number that he wrote down. That's all I have on him. This account can only be accessed by the signature placed on the system of the banks computer sir."

The police were gutted as they knew they had been outsmarted but it was too late. They had killed the minder and said he was shooting at them, which was a bluff and the mob boss had now been allowed to transfer onto witness protection but he had witnessed the shooting of the minder, so what could the police do?

Their hands were tied and to arrest Mr Nice now would stop the investigations on the drug smuggling there and then. So, others would then slip the net ready to become bigger but they wanted us all that were involved. Even if he could prove the money was legit, they knew it was dirty and would make them look silly again if they arrested him on this little evidence.

So, the Judge said he wanted the whole Firm banged to rights on the smuggling ring as the Judge had said there had been a witness on the boat when they had dived for it, when Mr B and he had got nicked in Southend. He knew there was a lot more to the whole organisation and he wanted them all behind bars.

The police drove off in the unmarked police van once they got back to the station and had got the mob boss off into witness protection. He told the other police on the case and the international police who too were now fuming and had now realised they had been outsmarted. They continued by telling the Judge who also wasn't happy even though he already knew what had happened.

So, ordered intense surveillance to be placed on Mr Nice and to wait until the money was signed for, then they would arrest him in the bank and that would make the link and they would all be in place ready to bust the whole Firm.

Don F was now on witness protection he was no good to them or anyone anymore. He had outsmarted them. What could they do now? Their cover had been blown. So they concentrated on Mr Nice with their investigation, as if they started rustling too many feathers the big ten year investigation that the Judge and the International serious crime squad had set up would go down the pan.

They had to tread carefully around Mr Nice until they had a closed case on him and the rest of the Firm. If they acted now with the little evidence they had, it could clue them all up and undo all the Judges hard work, which was to get all the Firm in custody and all the dirty cash they had accumulated with all the work they had done together over the last few years into the police vaults and bank accounts and be used for the fight against drugs and stopping their connections any way he could. And maybe he could treat himself to a nice holiday, if he could get his hands on some of it, which of course was the intention. Everyone in any form of power is a touch corrupt, or so it would seemed!

Things had to be done like this. They could trace the money from the bank and follow it back to the connections of the mob boss then they would have them bang to rights too and could then have them all in custody for laundering but it had been signed over to Mr Nice now as they had found out when they tried to go in and get it all with the informer the Italian man that had turned grass and was once on the list for signing over the money the police now they knew what he had done. So, he was now arrested and put in prison.

The Judge knew that Don F's money could be transferred at any time to anywhere in the world and they wouldn't be able to get it even if they tracked it as it might go to a benefactor that could warrant having this much then the trail would go cold. The Judge used his powers and ordered a staged robbery on the bank with some off-duty police officers to get the money out and in the police's hands before it went out the bank and was lost and shared equally amongst the underworld.

CHAPTER 26

So, the next day the off-duty Old Bill agents were briefed for this job. Two hours later they went crashing into the bank, staging the robbery and taking every penny in there so that it could be used again in the fight against crime.

The money that was legit was given back to the bank by the police as they had said they had caught the crooks. They had said they had caught up with the villains and have been able to retrieve their money but the money in the other account they couldn't get it back. So, they had only taken the dirty money that was in the account that they couldn't access. We later found out the killing of the minder and the mob boss was done by the other family members allegedly, as the police had smoothed it over and made it all look good in their enquiries.

Even though the Judge knew it was him and the police that's what they had said once interviewed by the local papers. This Italian member of the Firm had been caught and turned Bert smalls he had been caught on a charge of murder and whilst in court it had come out that he had been cheating with the main Sicilian mob boss's wife.

So he got his mate, this Judge he knew in England, involved even though he was involved in all their cases anyway unbeknown to them and Mr Nice and he was gathering as much as he could on them all so he could definitely put them all away for a long time and get the money back they had made out of all their immoral gains. Mr Nice, the Firm and both families that they all seemed to be connected to the Sicilian mob member had told all to this Judge just before the Judge had put him down and had told him about the money in the account.

The Sicilian mob member thought that the Italian man was shagging his wife and had doubts on his loyalty. So he had him killed. They said he had gone nuts and helped the Judge, that's why the Sicilian mob man, the one that Mr nice had met had now been put on witness protection.

The English Judge was able to do all this by the backing of an MP in London as he wanted the streets cleaned of these gangsters and thugs and organised crime for his election and he gave the power for the Judge to work in these ways of just bending the rules without raising any questions as they wanted drugs coming in under their control, not gangsters.

They wanted the streets clean but they also knew drugs created jobs and if they wanted to stop it all coming over they could. He had also employed undercover agents and bought back retired coppers to help to disrupt this criminal empire and their activities any way he could. Even if it meant killing certain powerful figures that were proving difficult to stop in the drug game; the hierarchy, not the street soldiers.

They had their fingers in many pies and had now corrupted higher government figures in their country and others in the underworld or that were connected to organised crime such as this. The MP thought that a lot of the money that was being made from the untouchable drug empires was now also being used to fund terrorism and he thought if he could make a big hole in the drug trade he may be able to stop the terrorists getting money to back themselves.

If he could pull it off then he would definitely be elected for prime minister and their power would be given to them to govern in the election. So, with their English judges help, backed by this MP, he had made the police hit the bank as they were told to get the dirty money back into the police vaults and the family man, the Sicilian mob boss retired and grassed the rest of the mob up.

The grass had clued him up to let him off a few things but now the murder he had to go down unless he came clean, so he did, but he had outsmarted them with the money.

But now the judge had it back? Mr Nice and Wong were sitting there in the café when they heard the explosion of the Four By Four coming off the road they saw the white van coming off the road as it swerved to make it look like it was an accident and to anyone else it had looked like a real accident.

Fuck two days.

"Let's go Wong."

Two days passed and Mr Nice went to the bank. He stopped outside as he pulled up.

He could see the police all around it and when he went to the bank he realised what had happened. The police were sniffing around it and he had to leave the money and the account, the whole two million of it, as it had been nicked.

Otherwise, he too would be inside. If he had made a fuss then he would have brought the attention he didn't want to himself but the police would want as they then knew for sure that Mr Nice would be their man. He was very fucking unhappy but very lucky. The police now had found out the money had been signed over to Mr Nice, but every last note was now in their custody.

So, that was the next piece to their puzzle and another notch on the police's belt to make the evidence overwhelming for Mr Nice once they were ready to pull him in and arrest the whole lot of his Firm including yours truly!

Once the unforeseen circumstances had passed, Mr Nice started having a look through the property magazine that he had picked up as the coffee came to their table after all the commotion. He still had some money stashed away. Enough to get the villa he wanted with his own drug business but he knew soon he would have to cut his ties with the Sicilian mob.

They were getting too hot to work with and so were the bank now the police were sniffing around it. The whole thing was getting too messy and it looked like it was coming on top for them and if he wanted to stay out of prison it was best to stay away and cut his ties for now like they had said to him to do. Mr Nice asked Wong how things were back in London.

"They're ok Mr Nice, but London isn't what it used to be when you were there. It's changing and changing fast now Johnny's gone. So are the people changing there too mate."

"Why's that Wong?" Mr Nice asked.

"Well, it's all multicultural now. The clubs and doors are being taken over by different nationalities and it seems that the Russians are starting to move in too and now have started running things. They seem to be behind more and more businesses nowadays. We have no choice but to let them do it. The police are getting more and more cameras everywhere and more money for undercover cops and the technology they have and are using now is unbelievable. You can't hide anywhere without a camera spotting you at least once. Wherever you go and every time you use your phone you can be tracked or they can listen in. It just isn't like the old days, even though Malcolm's there taking care of business. I know you come over now and then for the races at Ascot but you're only around for four days and you stay away from everyone that is connected to you while you're there. So you may not have noticed the change that has happened."

Mr Nice laughed to himself.

"That's right Wong, the Russians are running things now."

"I have noticed my friend and indeed they are."

"The good thing is Wong, most of them work alongside me now, even though I'm not there. So there shouldn't be any dramas Wong. One word from me and everyone does as they're told. I have made some good contacts over there in Russia and in London too, and even bigger ones than when I was there before. So it's not a bad thing mate."

Wong looked very unhappy.

"Wong, listen mate, don't look so sad. Things can't be that bad for you, can they? My thinking is Wong, if you can't beat these people then join them."

"What?"

Wong looked at Mr Nice as if he had gone soft.

"Look, if you start fighting these people there's a chance you could lose and we don't want that, as it can be a bit embarrassing. Once you lose you're out of the game or dead. So, while everyone else is wasting their time fighting against each other for a piece of the pie I have done the right thing and joined them. The Russians can be very unrepentant and that's what you need on a good Firm. Five or six staunch fellas that don't mess about and with these at your side you would be like the Roman army. Just marching on forward as the Russians are. Men with no fear are militant but very loyal Wong."

"So it's all good?"

"What's up Wong you look a bit taken aback by it all?"

"Well this Turkish Firm in London have used brute force to take over most of the fast food shops and the taxi ranks and whilst at it my friend's club doors too and this massage parlour. They keep robbing the tills and scaring the girls just being thugs, bullies really. My pal ain't having much success getting any of them back as 'Jimmy the Greek' as he is known to his friends and his brother has taken pretty much every massage parlour over now. Or has his fingers in it somehow. So it's under his control and he is working closely with the Albanians as they seem to be bringing all the women over here pushing the regular willing women workers out the way and pimping their own girls out there. This Turkish Jimmy has got himself into many pies from debt collecting to night club security and racketeering to protection schemes and he's got his hooks into my pal's two massage parlours and all sorts of other stuff." Wong paused for breath, "This Turkish geezer supplies the girls that will do anything and I mean anything and cheaper than the normal girls as they need the money. They're bought over with nothing. So they have no choice but to work. The Albanians like this so they look out for Jimmy. Fast food, taxis, you name it. His name is now behind most things and now large shipments of heroin are coming over with his contacts and this means he will be working closely with the Asians. Then we will have trouble on our hands. His name has even started to come to light on bigger Firms' lips that have been established for a long time in and around London. He seems to be working his way up the ladder fast as the heroin trade seems to be getting bigger and bigger. Even the other two big family Firms that run parts of London have his name marked but they are sitting in prison and can't do much right now."

Mr Nice interrupted.

"So, that's a good thing Wong, as within time, hopefully they will get rid of him and his crew of thugs and then you'll have no worries. Your little headache will be over."

"Well wish it were as easy as that."

"Wong, look you know some naughty people. You don't need me to get involved in your little domestics. Why not sort them out yourself? What about your minder, can she help?"

"Well I had the Triads come over for a few days as you know Yang, my minder, goes out with one of them and they track down his brother and cut him for a little warning but that didn't stop him. Or the rest of his crew of thugs. The Triads are responsible for protection and enforcing the Chinese community, not to do my personal work. They only want to be involved in immigrant smuggling and heroin importing. So that's why they have been so lenient with Jimmy as once he joins shoulders with the Asians then he will be getting heroin over a lot cheaper and they don't want to get involved in a personal feud as they have enough on their plates right now and there main concern is how China town is keeping, not Jimmy as I have found out. He is now doing small businesses with some of them too and like they said, unless he touches China town then they don't want to know. When I had a little chat with them, Jimmy and his thugs, he didn't want to listen and they seem to be getting bigger every day that goes passed. As they are now starting to do a lot of business with the Asians and I mean there has been talks for a lot of gear coming over and they too don't mess about. The Triads said if they touch China town then they will intervene but until then, it's not their problem and they will continue to trade with them. So, why get involved in others drama they said after they cut Jimmy's brother for a little warning not to come onto their turf. They told me that people who put their noses in other people's business normally get hurt. I know if Johnny was here then it would all be sorted out by now but he ain't so I have to sit back and let this happen. So, do you think I should stay out of it and let my friend deal with his own problems? Is that what you think Mr Nice?"

"Yes Wong," Mr Nice said. "Sometimes it's a lot less grief if you keep out of things unless they do really concern you."

Wong interrupted.

"But he has been a good friend to me before I met up with you. So I would like to help him, there's nothing wrong in that. I was on the run once for strangling a girl by accident in a sex game and I had to stab the pimp after he wanted paying and came in to the room and realized what had happened. It was an accident but he was having none of it. My friend hid me for one year before I got birded off for it and that's when I met you."

"Okay, after Yang, my minder, cut his brother for me just for a little warning he still hasn't listened and persisted. As long as he stays away from China town then he is safe and my hands are tied. Unless you can sort something out Mr Nice as he is protected by the Triads at the moment as he is now doing what he likes. Why hasn't Malcolm done anything for you?"

"He too said that he has his own problems to deal with and he doesn't want The Old Bill on his case. He is too busy collecting the money in to worry about this lot and I think they could turn out to be a bit heavy for Malcolm. Well I guess that's fair enough from the Triads after all what would they gain from it in the long run?"

"Nothing."

"Exactly. In this game no-one does anything for nothing Wong."

"Can't the Firm do me a little favour after all I have done for it?" asked Wong. "I think a little warning is needed Mr Nice."

"No Wong." Mr Nice said. "What's needed here isn't a warning, they seem like they have had that off your friends by what you have just told me and it didn't seem to work as they have been bought by him by the sounds of it. What's needed here Wong is a public warning, some action. Something needs to happen to shake them all up and make them stand up straight to get them to start minding and using their Ps and Qs and doing as they're told again. We're all gangsters round here Wong. You need to show them who they're fucking with. Get this Jimmy on the phone Wong ... Let me have a little whisper in his ear. I take it you have his number?"

"Yes."

"Okay."

Wong then took the phone out of his pocket.

"He won't listen to you or anyone Mr Nice. He has got too big for all that talking stuff."

"Tell me more about him, Wong. What is he all about? What about his family? I'll send someone round there."

"They're all involved Mr Nice. He was running a few

restaurants then moved onto a club that his brother had and now he is running his brothers door business and he has taken over some of the massage parlours my pal owns and the doors of the club and they are becoming more and more successful. Right now any manager that don't like them taking over their door has to suffer. Then the doormen have no choice but to join forces with Jimmy and before long they have taken over another door and another club. What they do causes problems in the club. Then they talk to the managers and say they will sort it for a nice drink and if it happens again will send our boys out to protect them as it seems the door staff now are struggling to keep the place safe and if it keeps happening they will then man your doors so before long they have taken a nice drink and taken another club over. They also go round to all the working girls places and rob them. Then some talk to the owners and say 'Look put our girls in there and we'll make sure the girls are safe and we want a nice percent paid to us on them.' So they get all the money and the girls that they bring over just get enough for food and board. That's how they work and treat them. They scare the girls half to death and then they say will protect them for a little fee of what they make. Then they move in on them and before long they own them too or are taking a wage out of the girl's earnings and the maids and the owners of the escort agencies have then been pushed out of business. They're sucking everyone dry."

"Okay, I hear what you say Wong. This has to stop. Before they take more. Ok, if it's upsetting you this much then I will help you."

"Mr Nice," says Wong. "It sounds like he's becoming a disease and we have to find a cure and I think I have just found it."

"Now give him a tinkle. It seems now that Johnny is gone people think they can do as they please."

Wong then called Jimmy for Mr Nice.

"Hello? It's me, Wong."

"Fuck off mate. I'm telling you the same as I told your mates, we run these businesses now. Your time has passed so move on. Piss off and keep your nose out of things that don't concern you. You'll have to kill us all before we listen to your lot and you'll find your restaurant on fire before you could say prawn fucking crackers if you keep on Wong. Now fuck off and stop bothering me."

Then the phone went dead.

"See," Wong moaned, "He just won't listen and if you don't care about dying then how you can teach them to listen or get them to do as they're told."

"Cheeky little Turkish fucker," said Mr Nice, "He ain't your average Turkish delight now is he? Where would they be right now Wong?"

"I'm not sure. I know they own loads of cab shops and this club and pub in Kilburn and some of their boys will be at the massage parlour now. In London they have control of two opposite each other which were my pal's once. The others I'm not too bothered with. The King James pub is where most of them meet before they go on to work."

"Okay, so they'll be there now then will they?"

Wong looked at his watch.

"Yes, I think so. They all meet at this pub after they have been to the baths just before they all go off for their work. Some will be at Stacy's' massage parlour just off the Kilburn high road. Let me phone my friend to find out."

He rang his friend and got him to walk past the pub and then went and had a massage.

"Yes. They're all here Wong."

"Thanks mate, be home soon."

"Okay."

"Just need to sort things out here in Marbella and I'll be back and I'll get this mess sorted for you. Look, I will not let you down I will get your place back for you just calm yourself. It's all in good hands then we'll call it a day.

"Mate, they're all in the pub and at Sandy's and Stacy's massage parlour." Wong confirmed as he said bye to his friend on the phone.

"Ok," Mr Nice picked up his phone and left the table. "Give me two seconds Wong. I'll be back in a bit. I just need to think for a second."

He wanted to arrange some things out of earshot of Mr Wong.

CHAPTER 27

I now found myself sitting in an Escort convertible with two genetically engineered ex KGB mercenaries whose deadly efficiency was now needed.

We were waiting outside some moody looking pub in Kilburn waiting for Wong's call, just as Mr Nice had said he would.

Mr Nice had rung Old School and he had clued Old School up and in return he had phoned me up about one hour before to say he would be ringing soon and to go see Hector who then would give me these two Russians I was now sitting with awaiting orders. They didn't say much and didn't have to. They scared the shit out of me and I'm sure few others had been allowed to get this close to them without dying.

Mr Nice then went back to the table and said, "Do me a favour Wong, ring Jimmy again."

"What's the point Mr Nice? You heard him."

"Just do it will you?"

The phone rang.

"Here, give me the phone Wong."

Wong handed him the phone.

"Hello Jimmy."

"Who's this?"

"No mate. You listen to me, names ain't important right now. What is important is that you live to see your Grandchildren. If I were you, I would get all your doormen off the doors and away from any clubs in London or massage parlours. I don't play at being a gangster. I am a fucking gangster. And let it be known to you all, I don't abide by any of the old codes that you lot seem to be playing lip service too. I make the rules in London and if it takes me to get rid of every single one of you then mark my words I shall. So, before it all ends in tears and you are all resting in the garden of peace do me a favour and do the right thing my little Turkish friend and get the fuck out of it or at least from the two massage parlours and off the factory night club as they belong to good friends of mine. So, while you still can, I would get it done ASAP. Have I made myself clear son? Stick to the kebab shops and the taxis and everything will be hunky-dory."

"Bollocks you English bastard. Who is this? I will come and cut your tongue out and serve it up in a pitta bread."

Jimmy put the phone down.

He was sat in the pub with his little mob giving it large. Being all cocky.

"Who's that Jimmy?" asked his brother.

"Some English bastard that thinks he's bulletproof and that I should listen to him. He wants me out of London and off the doors of the Factory night club and the two massage parlours in particular. Don't worry, I hear it all the time. People making empty threats. It's that Wong now. He knows we are connected to the Triads. His ace card has just been jumped."

"So, what was he saying?" his brother asked.

"He's only got someone threatening me and they are say they're coming to kill me, but they won't. Wait till we finally make the Asian connection in Bradford. Then no one will be talking. The only talk will be about us."

"Yes mate, phone the Cookster up," Mr Nice said to Wong.

"What's he going to do?" He dialled the number.

So, here I was in the car with these two Russian mercenaries outside the pub in Kilburn as the call came through to me.

I picked up the phone as it rang.

"Hello?" I glanced at the pub as two nice looking women left it.

Then I looked back again in my mirror to see these two staunch fellas staring at me in the back seat of the car.

"It's Wong."

"Wong, yes Mate. How you doing? It's been a long time mate."

"Here give me the phone," Mr Nice instructed Wong, "Cookster!" he shouted down the phone.

"Yes Mr Nice?" I recognised his deep London gangster's accent.

"It's me son, and it's time you showed these fellas that are sitting in the pub the ways of the Firm. I hope that you are now outside with some friends of mine and Hector's. By my book son, you should now be sitting ready to fly the flag for the Firm once again. Are you there or are you once again wasting the Firm's time?"

"Yes. Mr Nice I am here and they are here with me."

"Okay son, without further ado tell them to let them have it."

"Okay."

The phone went dead. I turned round to the two Russians.

"Okay fellas, do your worst."

They then bent down opened their bags and put on their shower caps and their leather gloves and then put ear plugs up their noses and placed balaclavas on their heads. I put mine on too. They were wearing their white painting jump suits.

They then unzipped the bags in front of them and pulled out the tools. They had placed a bag around the case of their SMG to collect and stop the bullet shells from coming out all over the place in the car or onto the floor. They then in unison pulled the bolts back on their sub machine guns to cock them ready and then told me to let the roof down.

As the roof slowly reclined and came to a rest and clipped into place they looked at each other and nodded and both of them sprang up into action.

They both jump up in unison and position themselves as fast as they could at the back of the motor and then, with fingers on the triggers, they start firing as the guns rattled into action.

As the fellas in the pub sat down to talk business to Jimmy, the fella Mr Nice had just spoken to, he looked out of the window and all in slow motion out of the corner of his eye he saw the two Russian mercenaries stand up from the car. Jimmy shouted, "Shit, get the fuck down!" as he dropped his beer. Then as the beer hit the floor and the glass smashed and the beer came rushing out of the broken glass Jimmy dove under the table to try to shield himself that bit more.

Everyone looked around at each other to see what the

commotion was. Then they turned as bullets started raining in through the pub window. Passing and penetrating the window of the pub all in slow motion and other parts of it as the bullets came raining in, hitting people at random as the two Russian mercenaries spewed the entire contents of their two sub machine guns into the pub window. They were hitting all different things at random and they smashed up bottles and glasses and were hitting people who then dropped to the floor or slumped onto the tables. These people that were getting hit belonged to Jimmy's little crew. The guns stopped rattling off their bullets and the gun's bolts clicked into place. So the two Russian mercenaries both turned round and sat down and spoke calmly.

"Move now."

I pushed my foot to the metal and stared into space in disbelief at what I had just seen. We wheel spun out of there and once out of sight they removed the bags from the guns. They had collected the shells nicely in the bags and then removed their balaclavas and I then pulled mine off. We were out of there. I was shaking at what I had seen.

Mr Nice looked at the clock.

"Ring him again."

"Who?"

"That Jimmy. The fella that was giving you a hard time. See if he's changed his tune yet."

Mr Nice sipped at his coffee.

"I doubt it. I bet he don't even answer this time round mate."

"Well," Mr Nice said, "He may not be able to."

"If he doesn't answer then I know he has lost his bottle. If he doesn't and he's all mouth and no action Wong. He must be a very lucky man if he does answer Wong."

"What?" Wong said, a bit confused,

"You know the one giving your mates club and the parlours a hard time and who keeps disrespecting you. Get him back on the phone. Give him a call."

"He won't listen to me. So you're wasting your time keep phoning him Mr Nice."

"I said ring him again Wong. Look give me the fucking phone." Mr Nice started to turn a bit more forceful as Wong looked at him, "Just give me the phone."

Wong pulled the phone out and gave it to Mr Nice.

"All the calls in the world ain't going to sort it out Mr Nice. What we need is some action as you said just a little while ago."

Mr Nice rang the number once again. It rang but no answer. He left it ringing for a bit.

"Sounds like it's all done mate."

"What is?" Wong says.

CHAPTER 28

Jimmy was now laying on the floor shitting his pants and looking a bit uncomfortable curled up in a ball. He couldn't believe what he had just witnessed. He had his hands over his head quivering like a babe. Covering his head he now had blood all over him but it was not his own. He then looked around, then up and out of the smashed windows. He then looked all around him again and saw his friends all shot with blood coming out of their bullet wounds amongst the carnage. He was in shock.

"No. No. No."

Then he heard the phone ring as he came out of his shock. He saw his phone lying on the floor as it started to ring again and vibrate. He then leaned over and picked it up, a bit shaken and slowly pushed the answer button.

"Err ... Yes?"

Mr Nice walked out the café and out of earshot of everyone else in the café. He put his hand around the mouth piece of the phone, cupping it to make his voice sound more menacing than it already was.

"Still alive then? You must be a cat as they have nine

lives too."

"What?" Jimmy said, confused.

"I told you it would all end in tears. Don't fuck with me otherwise your all dead and right about now you must be a very lucky man to still be here chatting to me. By rights you of all people should be dead already."

Jimmy was lost for words.

"So, now I have your attention and you know I don't fuck about. Are you listening to me?"

"Yes," Jimmy stuttered, as he looked at his pals all shot to pieces with the holes in their bodies pouring with blood.

"Get off the Factory nightclub doors and leave the two parlours alone that Mr Wong has shown an interest in. Get your men and women out of the parlours and stick to driving people around London. Do you hear me? Because it won't take me long to find you and if I have to I will."

Mr Nice put the phone down.

Jimmy looked around at the carnage and phoned his head doorman to tell them that it was all over and that they were now out of work, otherwise they may find themselves dead.

"What? Jimmy, you can't do that."

"I just have. It's no more. I'm out of business I am handing it all over to a fella called Old School who will be in contact with you all soon. I am going back to just doing the restaurants and the cabbing. If you want to be a part of that then that's great. If not then you're on your own looking for work, as you are no longer employed by me. I don't want any more blood on my hands. I have let the club go and the parlours."

"Why? What's up Jimmy?"

"Look, I've fucking sold them all ok? So find another fucking job."

He hung up, then phoned Mr Nice straight back.

"Okay, it's done. I'll send someone for you to put them back into the rightful owner's name. The fella coming or who will in time come to see you will be called Old School."

"Wise move my friend," said Mr Nice Firmly, "This is nothing personal. Just when people step out of turn they need to be told. And if they don't listen the first time round then they have to be taught to listen. Okay?"

"Okay. I respect that."

"Make sure you do as when I see you, and I'm sure I will one day, I'd like extra salad in my kebabs Okay? Otherwise you'll have a bullet in the back of your nut and you won't know where it's come from until they fish you out of the Thames."

Jimmy knew he had just paid the price for overstepping the mark as there is always someone bigger and more able up the ladder than yourself and if he wanted to live he had no choice but to do as Mr Nice had told him. He knew he was lucky and that his luck had just come to an end as it always does as he looked at the carnage in the pub.

Jimmy's door empire had just come crashing down like a pack of cards in one quick swoop. The Factory nightclub was now given back to Wong's friend Nick. Wong was given a nice drink for Mr Nice's work once he got back to London.

The phone went dead just as the police, the ambulance and the armed police arrived at the pub where they found them all lying on the floor with Jimmy. The witnesses were saying nothing to the police. When they were asking the survivors questions not many people were letting too much out, only a few eye witnesses said they saw three masked men in a car emptying their guns.

CHAPTER 29

I parked the car up next to the Maserati where Hector was waiting with the engine running, just next to Epping Forest in Essex, on our return once the hit was done.

The two Russians jumped out of the car as I poured petrol all over it like they told me to. They then took off their gloves and jumpsuits off to reveal their smart, crisp-cut, expensive, tailor-made suits. Then they threw their jumpsuits into the fire as the car went up in flames. They then placed the guns into their cases in the boot of Hector's car and then buried the bullet shells a bit further up, in the mud in the forest, as Hector drove up a bit more back onto the main road. When all this was done we moved on to the next stage of the plan.

"To the parlours," one of the Russians said.

Hector nodded and we then drove slowly, creeping out of the wood's track road back onto the road and headed into the streets of London. No one said a word to anyone else.

Before long we were outside the two massage parlours in London. The two Russian hit men got out in unison, one out of the left side of the car and one out of the right side.

They then walked into the parlours, one on the left and the other on the right side of the road. As they walk in and up the stairs one of them knocked on the door with the signs saying, 'Hot, sexy, blond model ready and waiting.' A lady opened the door.

"She is very busy darling, but you can come in and wait."

The hit men could see Jimmy's man inside, reading the newspaper, through the crack in the door. He pulled the girl to him and pulled out his gun with the silencer on.

Jimmy's guard dropped the paper a little to see what was going on. He then stood up to come to her aid but the Russian mercenary head-butted him and kicked him into the chair and then pulled the trigger, hitting the fella once in the chest on his way down. He fell back onto the settee with the paper over his head. The Russian then locked the lady in the room with the working girl and the punter and told them not to leave the room until someone let them out. Then he placed the gun in his suit, shut the door and walked calmly back outside.

As he walked down the stairs another man came up the stairs.

"She's busy mate."

"Oh, thanks." The man turned around and they both came down and out onto the street together. The Russian got into the Maserati.

The other Russian killer knocked on the door of the parlour across the road. As the guard opened it, he got a glimpse of the Russian's gun and he realised what was happening. He quickly tried to shut the door. The Russian kicked it and the door swung open. He raised his gun and let him have it as the door sprung back shut. You could hear a body flump onto the floor and the screams of the working girl as she came out to see the dead man on the floor with the maid. The Russian hit man then placed the gun into his inside pouch and walked down the stairs and got into the other side of the car. They had let the guards have it there and then all within five minutes of getting out of the car.

"Let's go, it's all done." the Russian said to Hector as he drove off slowly, not bringing attention to themselves as they drove off. We were all in silence again until Hector rang Old School to then go into the parlours to get rid of the bodies in the big rubbish bins out the back, So that George the dustbin man could come collect them and bury them under a tonne of rubbish at the rubbish site that day.

Old School clued the girls up and said they were free to go as long as they said nothing. One of their girls were being forced to work there and she was thankful to Old School for letting her go and be reunited with her family. They agreed and so they left and Old School spoke to Wong's friend and got back the original girls that wanted to work in there as he had handed their control back over to Wong's friend.

Now, things would go back to how they were before Jimmy and his bullies came on the scene. Old School even let the girls that were being held there go and only let girls work in them if they chose too. The girls were happy once again and kissed Old School and couldn't thank him enough even though it was Mr Nice's planning that had made this all happen. Old School took most of the credit from the girls as they were none the wiser.

"Thanks Old School."

"No problem girls."

He then put female maids in there to run the gaffs that worked for him and Wong's mate. The fella that owned the two parlours wiped Mr Wong's big card debts off for his help, unbeknown to Mr Nice as he had got himself a debt on the games of backgammon they were playing some nights in the restaurant.

Wong would have paid it off once he had made it back on Mr Nice's drug money but now he had done this for his mate he had wiped the debt was eradicated, one less thing to stress about! Hector and I then took the Russian hit men back to the airport. Death was their business and right now business was booming for them as they had just killed five of Jimmy's crew in just five hours of being here in England.

Hector had taken care of the guns and had put them back in the ceiling of a garage toilet that was always locked as his girlfriend's friends' pad Hector paid her good money to keep them locked up there. No one knew that they were concealed in the false toilet roof so next time you take a piss, there may just be two machine guns above your head. The police were always at the pub in Kilburn and it was on the ten o'clock news and on Crime Watch but no one had been caught for the murders yet. Hector was a very complex man with a ruthless core.

He had become entwined with Mr Nice and their financial matters in London and they were now both well linked to the Russian Mafia crime boss after Mr Nice helped them out. He also knew the yardie leader as he was going out with his daughter and his gang were responsible for most, if not all, of London's crack habit. The cocaine that was coming over from Mr Nice was now coming from them and to Old School through Old School's connections into their hands and they were then washing it into crack. But, Hector and the yardie boss daughter didn't get involved with all that and the politics that went with it all.

They stayed away.

CHAPTER 30

Now by sorting all this out Mr Nice had made more doors available to him than he had doormen working, as one other doormen had heard about other doormen getting killed they didn't want to risk being on the door as they knew they would be sitting ducks themselves. It meant we could all have free massages from the girls whenever we liked now they were free to run their own business and we would just take a percentage of their earnings from the main fella whose property they were renting out.

Not all of the girls themselves, but just a little bit of their day's earnings. So, for every one hundred pounds they earned, we would get thirty quid. That gave room for the Russian crime boss to send his people over here to work the doors for Mr Nice, and they were getting SIA badges for the doors with no problems as they all had a clean fresh record over here. The good thing was they were all allowed SIA cards where the other bouncers from old were now being refused and that gave way to a new wave of gangsters as the Russians now worked the doors and had joint shoulders with Mr Nice.

That's why everyone thought they had taken over, but only as Mr Nice was rubbing shoulders with the Russian Mafia's crime boss and his people were very loyal and didn't mess around. That, and a few other things which are best not talked about, is more or less how the Russian connection were born in London, thanks to Hector and Mr Nice and some other deals with the Colombians and the Sicilian mob that are best not talked about for the safety of the author.

To be continued …